I0187191

SMOKING
THE PIPE OF
CONTEMPLATION

Road to Revelation

VOLUME 1

RICHARD BARTRAND

BARTRAND
B O O K S

i

D E D I C A T I O N

To the seeking souls

I dedicate this book to those who are in search of truth, peace, and unity in an endless sea of tainted information. Those who wrestle with their daily demons and dragons with no end in sight. Some may have most things together but feel deep in their soul that there's more out there than what meets the eye.

Before you get trapped in the endless cycles of painful routine, or if that's already an established grind, take the information in this book to break free from this merry-go-round delusion that life is a giant bag of nonsense, inevitably throwing you into the next wind of happenstance ... over and over again until you cross the finish line, only to find out it was the grave.

It's been my goal to uncover the hidden things of life and dig down to the bedrock of understanding; to uncover the original divine design for humanity, if you will, and to set at ease the minds of those who are also seeking the truth no matter where it leads. It's a long and painful journey sometimes, but the result will be a resting place for your soul. This isn't a book of religion. Those who know me know that I'm not a big fan of religion and will speak about it almost every chance I get, but I will also say this ... The architect, creator, and source of all living things has been hijacked and manipulated into multi-faceted religious institutions that chain you to a conditioned belief system rather than set you free to live.

This is not a persuasion towards changing your worldview or convictions. If you're already sold to your beliefs, this will only enhance your experiences inside those beliefs. If you're already dedicated to a cause, let these nuts and bolts make it a deeper one.

Table Of Contents

1. PERSONAL ADVICE   1

   * The Winds Of Change   2

   * Courageous Or Cowardice   3

   * Mental Roller-Coaster   6

   * Living In The Hypothetical   9

   * I Like This ... But   13

   * Indecision Is A Habit   18

   * Finding The Sweet Spot   22

   * Mental Death by Observation   29

   * T.D.H.D   36

   * Why Do We Give Up?   41

   * Try And Fail Or Do And Succeed   47

   * Is There Any Purpose to Your Depth of Suffering?   51

   * Worthless Emotional Energy   54

   * I Should ~VS~ I Will   60

   * Oil Your Happy Hinge With Gratitude   62

   * Interest Is The Gateway To Change   65

2. CONTROVERSIAL OBSERVATIONS   68

    ✷   Random Acts of Blindness   69

    ✷   Toxic Masculinity   77

    ✷   Pro-Life / Pro-Choice   79

    ✷   Hive Mind of (un)Social Media   85

    ✷   The Blinded Eyes Of Those Unwilling to See   88

    ✷   Rinse The Soap Out Of Your Brainwash   91

    ✷   Indoctrinated Prejudices   96

    ✷   Harsh Reality Of A Miserable Life   100

    ✷   This World Wasn't Made For You!   104

    ✷   LIFE SUCKS!   108

    ✷   Overpowering Deceptive Forces   113

3. POETRY COLLECTION   122

    ✷   Invisible Untapped Potential   123

    ✷   Silent Cries   125

    ✷   Keep Your Faith Until The End   127

    ✷   My Brothers Keeper   128

    ✷   Shackles Of Limitation   129

    ✷   Cycles Of Seeking Faith   131

    ✷   Real Life   133

    ✷   Turning Cold   135

    ✷   So What   136

    ✷   Absolute Power Is Mine   138

ABOUT THE AUTHOR   143

1
PERSONAL ADVICE

PHYSICAL ~ MENTAL ~ EMOTIONAL ~ RELATIONAL ~ SPIRITUAL

Random articles written from the archives of the mind

and lessons learned from living life:

Sometimes through careful observations:

Sometimes the hard way.

This section is a compilation of things I've learned from life and the realization that the "bad" times are what teach you the most, so when you finally embrace what life has to offer on both sides of the spectrum ... life reveals its meaning.

THE WINDS OF CHANGE

VOLUNTARY CHANGE = INVOLUNTARY REACTIONS

A massive voluntary change in yourself brings with it an equally involuntary change in those around you.

They will either embrace who you're becoming with open arms and encourage you to be the better you, or they will fight against your change because it means they might have to change as well ... and change is a scary thing for those who have grown accustomed to the comfort zone.

However, during any transformation, there's an adjustment period that can get ugly due to over or under-compensation in the process. Sometimes you hit your mark and sometimes you fall short, but eventually, things will reach an equilibrium.

Those who want to support your desire to always strive to become a better person will be patient and understanding along your journey and others will want to come with you, fight to keep you the same, or sever whatever ties they have with you.

These are natural steps in the process because not everyone is on the same journey as you. Let things play out the way they play out. Those who are supposed to be in your life will still be there for every level of transformation you achieve.

Courageous Or Cowardice

Where's the line?

The difference between the two, you will be surprised to know, is a very thin and quite adjustable line in the sand.
At first glance, the two may appear to be enormously different and stand on the complete opposite ends of the spectrum, but let's take a closer look to see if that stands true.

Courageous is the quality of being brave: the ability to face danger, difficulty, uncertainty, or pain without being overcome by fear or being deflected from a chosen course of action.

Cowardice is a lack of courage, an absence of courage, or cowardly behavior.

In those definitions it would suggest that they are indeed on both ends of the spectrum because cowardice is a "lack" of courage, and courage is embedded in the word courageous, so take out courage and you don't have the word courageous.

Follow me on this as I present a different outlook.

Courageous and cowardice, believe it or not, actually stand side by side. They crouch at the same starting line, their feet are standing at the same cliff ledge, and both have their hand on the same unopened doorknob.

Both are faced with the enemy of FEAR!

The fear of the unknown, the fear of failure, the fear of rejection or humiliation, the fear of, *"what if it doesn't turn out the way I want it to?"*

~ WHATEVER THE FEAR IS ~

The only difference is, they are attached to a different action.

- Cowardice, when faced with fear, backs down **BECAUSE** of fear.

- Courageous, when faced with the same fear, presses forward DESPITE the fear!

Fear itself is not the issue. It may be an obstacle but it's not the issue.

- Both are experiencing the same fears.

- Both are in the same place of being faced with the unknown and lack the foreknowledge of any outcome.

- Both are usually terrified by the thoughts of a negative outcome.

- Both have the same capacity for choice.

One chooses to let their reasons for success push them forward and the other lets their excuses for failure hold them back.

~ SO HERE'S A THOUGHT ~

The definition doesn't separate one from the other — action does!

If you do tend to back down because of fear, then choose it in the arena of fearing regret, or fearing the negative effects in your life that will result from not taking some action.

Fear itself IS NOT real, it is mostly made up of the negative conditioning in your mind, so start tweaking your thinking and make fear your new play toy.

Life is meant to live! Take some risks!

Drop your teddy bear off at the safe space
and leave a goodbye note.

One comes from abundance ... One comes from lack.

Courageous steps forward ... Cowardice steps back.

Mental Roller-Coaster

The Subconscious Prison

How are you doing?

I'm good. ~ OR ~ Life sucks.

Those two responses are usually based on the concept of;

I'm good ... because "THINGS" are good.
or
I'm bad ... because "THINGS" are bad.

Whatever your explanation is beyond that, depends on a conditional circumstance that you were programmed to react to because you subconsciously label that circumstance as either good or bad.

An Example would go something like this;

~ **I'm Good** ~ *Life's good because I'm getting along with everyone in my circle, my car is running well, my bills are paid, and my pet hasn't chewed my belongings into tiny pieces lately ... or;*

~ **I'm Bad** ~ *Life sucks because my spouse is a #@!%&*, my car* *broke down, I got an unexpected bill in the mail, I just got dumped by my boyfriend/girlfriend, or the weather is horrible.*

Question:

Did you know you can still be "good" and even "joyful" ... even if everything goes wrong? All you need to do is separate your emotional mood from those outside influences. What I mean by outside influences are the nouns that exist in the physical that reside outside you and interfere with your daily routine. The things that trigger the mental and emotional reactions.

There's a magical space between a circumstance and the reaction to that circumstance. You can re-program your reactions by consciously choosing to react differently from how you've been conditioned since birth.

It's only a choice away.

It's a pretty simple concept, however, from the time you choose to separate emotions from circumstances until you create new response habits, it's going to take reconditioning and practice but it's well worth the struggle.

Now comes the choice

You can either believe me and move past the roller-coaster

of emotions by choosing to BE GOOD no matter what your circumstances are.

Or

You can continue to be defined by your circumstances ... meaning you choose to "BE" bad when "THINGS" are bad and "BE" good when "THINGS" are good.

Whatever meaning you place on any circumstance is the attitude that follows that meaning.

So, if you choose to be joyful despite your surroundings, you can rise above the cesspool of negative emotions, breathe the fresh air of freedom, and drop the automatic habitual reactions you were influenced by.

LIVING IN THE HYPOTHETICAL

FROM "WHAT IF" TO "WHAT IS"

Think of it this way ... you're shortchanging yourself if something is "going wrong" and you worry about what will happen or what might happen instead of just living what is happening right now in this very moment, even though it may appear to be a bad thing to you.

For example;

If you have a loved one who has a terminal disease, such as cancer, and you're worried sick and overly sad that it might be their last year on planet Earth. You're not going to fully enjoy the last year you have with them because, on your part, you have your worry, stress, anxiety, and negative anticipation to contend with, as well as the disease itself on their part.

Here's the switch in mindset ... If you stop worrying about the **"what-ifs"** and enjoy the **"what is"** ... right here and right now, you'll take out all the obstacles to live that last year as best as possible for everyone involved.

> If it's going to happen anyway ...
> worrying doesn't prolong the inevitable.

Yes, this would be tragic news and a little setback deserving of deep thought and some extra planning, but my point is if you look at the facts, accept the truths, and readjust to them ...

- You will get control of your emotions instead of letting your emotions control you.

- You will do whatever you can inside of your abilities to make life comfortable for everyone involved.

- You won't let your attitude falter because of your circumstances, but keep a good attitude and move forward despite your circumstances.

- You'll develop the skills to move ahead of the situation with positive anticipation.

You might be thinking ... how am I supposed to remain positive when I'm witnessing my loved one suffering?

Let's look at this in two separate lights:
1. If everyone is sad and miserable because their loved one is suffering ... this makes that loved one feel burdened by causing everyone this universal grief, which snowballs into more grief and mental issues, such as grief, anxiety, stress, etc., can cause physical problems, making things much worse.

   The point ... your added stress, worry, anxiety, grief, sadness, and so on, will not only make things worse but, quite possibly, shorten the timeframe you have with them.

2. If everyone tries to make it a point to be positive and joyful because the situation itself and the attitude you choose to have are two separate issues, then the levels of stress, worry, or anxiety will naturally subside and the attitude in the room will be much better.

This does not mean that you are happy about the situation, it simply means you choose to be happy despite the situation.

Your upbeat attitude and positive demeanor will only make things better by setting the pace for everyone else in the room and, on the contrary, maybe even prolonging the time they have left because of the mood.

There is no way to predict the future, and for all you know, they may have another 10 years left and you would have spent those 10 years worried and stressed that every one of them might be the last.

Or ... you can be in a place that rests in the fact that you can't change when the end is, so you might as well make the best of it until it does happen.

This life is temporary. In every lifetime, nothing here on earth is going to last past your last breath anyway! Enjoy what you have right here, right now. Make the best of each situation, push forward, and don't dwell in the past, or worry about the future.

Live right now and live to the best of your abilities.
Always move forward!

I'm not downplaying any tragedy and I didn't say that it wouldn't be hard, but if you fall prey to letting your weaker human side get the best of you, as we all do from time to time ... leave the room, readjust, regain your composure and get back in the game with a smile.

Don't think for a second that because you have a smile on your face and a good attitude, that somehow it means you are happy about the situation because, let me say it again, your attitude and any given circumstance are two completely separate entities deserving of two completely separate attitudes.

This means you don't have to be happy about the event but you can be simultaneously happy, separate from that event.

Rise above your circumstances and play on a field that chooses to intentionally respond positively to life's little surprises and defy the normal negative reactions that some choose to reside in.

***

Live life until there's no life left to live.

I Like This ... But

I Also Like That

Our drive to "like" some things comes from a series of different outlooks we possess. Each thing can be closely related to the next, forming a chain of various beliefs that create similar actions. Each belief creates an equal action to that specific belief.

But there's a problem ...

On one side of the chain, the next link in the progression is very similar, but by the time you get to the end of the chain, in comparison, the first and last links can be as different as night and day. This causes a form of cognitive dissonance in the entire system as a whole.

For instance:
- We would "LIKE" to succeed in business endeavors and make a good living for ourselves.

- We would "LIKE" to be in a perfect relationship, to always get along and be in deep love with them to live the "happily ever after" life.

- We would "LIKE" to be the ultimate embodiment of our core selves as either masculine or feminine beings.

With this concept stretching out over all aspects of our desired projections in life, we subconsciously expect those likes to materialize with little success. So why is it we fail miserably in this quest for unadulterated perfection?

If I were to boil everything down to the short answer, it would be this; We also "LIKE" to kill an enormous amount of time doing things that counteract the "LIKES" listed above, and these opposing "LIKES" are what sabotage the desired "LIKES" that we would rather possess.

- We would like to be successful, but we also like to play video games and scroll for hours on social media.

- We would like to have a rather sizable bank account, but we also like to impulse shop for things we don't need.

- We would like to be disciplined in our chosen profession, if we even know what that is, but also like to amuse ourselves, parked on the couch in front of the T.V.

- We would like to have a tack-sharp, focused mind, but also like to indulge in mind-altering substances.

I'm sure this list is triggering a massive outpouring of comparisons that are flooding your mind right now, and no doubt it could be a separate book on its own ...

So ... what do we do about it?

First and foremost is the recognition between the two separate forms of "LIKES" and realizing they are fighting for dominance inside your subconscious, habitual mindset almost every second of the day. The act of recognizing them will pull them into your consciousness where you can act on them and do something about it.

Also, recognize the difference that one is long-term and one is short-term. We are almost always prone to choose the short-term because of a feeling called instant gratification. Mentally, they would rather go out to a fast-food restaurant rather than spend time preparing a healthier home-cooked meal.

The quickest way to differentiate between the two is to make a solid, conscious decision to, from this point forward, stop yourself whenever you choose to settle for the lesser of the two.

Continuously ask yourself the tougher questions, like:

1. Is this a short-term, selfish, unhealthy, self-sabotaging, I quit, time-killing, entertaining, unproductive ... instant gratifying, "LIKE"? ~ Or

2. Is this a long-term, selfless, healthy, self-preserving, keep going, investment, educational, productive ... patient, "LIKE"?

Have you noticed that almost every one of the short-term results;
- Leaves you wanting more?

- Pacifies you with a temporary feeling?

- Never satisfies your deepest genuine desires?

- Never brings you to a place of lasting peace or something to be proud of?

Only the long-term goals that you've reached through dedication and hard work will ever satisfy the deeper parts of your soul.

The temporal carnal desires, otherwise known as the "flesh" will always try to get you to focus on the instant gratification or the "short-term" ~ here and now. The path that renders a temporary hollow outcome.

The permanent pure desires come from our true selves, known as the "spirit" which will always try to get you to focus on the delayed gratification or the "long-term" path to patience. The path that renders a deep, lasting peace.

Once you master the art of separating the two ... consciously and continuously choosing to act on the most productive "LIKES", and disciplining yourself to, at least, significantly reduce instant gratification to where it's inside your control, you won't automatically fall back into a state of insecurity and bondage as much. Eventually, creating new and better habits.

If you're thinking right now that this seems like a lot of work that can't be accomplished by someone as "weak" as you ...

or so you tell yourself ...

This is the voice of instant gratification speaking through your submission to the habitual subconscious. In other words ... it's a bad habit. Like smoking, drug use, or excessive drinking ... habits can be broken ... and will be broken by creating better habits.

All habits are not bad.

You are perfectly capable of being a habitual non-smoker, a habitually fluent violinist, or an extremely successful business owner through practicing the routines necessary to get there ... which is creating the habit of successful business practices or filling yourself with the knowledge and actions of a professional musician.

Instead of reaching for a cigarette, reinforcing the bad habit ... Instead, reach for a book to create a new, better one.

Every time you recognize another bad habit, whether it be mental, physical, emotional, financial, vocational, social, spiritual, etc. ... Make a note of it and immediately think of ways to replace it with a more productive, positive, better way to think or act, and then put it into action.

Eventually, your life will become what you want, in light of the "Likes" that you deeply and truly desire.

It's just a simple matter of trading one habit for another.

INDECISION IS A HABIT

HABITS CAN BE BROKEN

If you have trouble making up your mind, you have been unrealistically practicing perfectionism to some degree or you're trying to project a flawless outcome with no forward action.

In other words, trying to predict every possible conclusion with pinpoint accuracy ~ just by thinking about it alone ~ will only keep you in a holding pattern; flying in circles until you figure out how to land the plane without crashing ... but you'll never figure that out until you put your tires to the pavement and land.
Eventually, this will happen anyway. You will keep flying in circles until you run out of fuel and be forced to land the plane whether or not you're ready. You might as well attempt to land with some fuel left in case you have to throttle back up to correct your course.

In comparison, that analogy can apply to every decision in life that you have to make up your mind for, so if you are indecisive, it was more than likely learned from an influence of yours when you were developing your cognitive skills. Then you just kept acting out indecisiveness until it was nothing more than a bad habit.

~ Practice Deciding ~

Yes, it's a practice, like juggling. You will never learn how to juggle until you drop quite a few balls. Start small to build confidence, but start somewhere. Take action on whatever thoughts you feel could make a positive difference in either your or someone else's life. Take a chance at doing something a little risky. Start a side business. Who knows, it might just turn into your own company.

When a thought comes to mind, instead of trying to over-analyze it 387 times before you decide to do anything about it, DO some kind of action toward that thought rather than just thinking about it.

Invest in something and make that something ... YOU!

Put some legs on those thoughts and take the first step towards it. Once that one is done, take the next one. Nobody ever knows the end game conclusion to anything and most of the time you won't even know the outcome of your first step, but I can tell you this ... you'll get nowhere just thinking about it.

Let's get this out of the way ...

No, not everything is going to work out the way you expected. You're not always going to succeed, and you, more than likely, are going to lose a bit of time and money in the process.

Hey, if anything else, you just learned what not to do next time. Get back in the game and try again ... and again ... and again ... until you DO succeed.

That, my friends, is a recipe for success.

JUST DO IT!

I started this article out with the words ***"Indecision is a habit"*** because it popped into my head without knowing what to write after that, but as soon as I wrote the title, more words came to mind, so I wrote those down too.

What you've read so far has been a series of words strung together, one thought at a time, and one action to that thought until the sentence you just read was formed, which, by the way, wasn't planned when I started this paragraph. It just kept building on the last thought, word, sentence, paragraph, and eventually, an entire article.

Don't stop there ... that article could be part of a chapter, and that chapter could then turn into a book.

The point is that you can apply this concept to everything in life. Relationships, business, outreaches, organizations, writing, photography, travel ... the list is endless.

So what are you waiting for? Pick a thought, sit down, and plan as far as you can, leaving your unrealistic expectations of understanding how it's all going to play out right off the list. You'll figure that out along the way. Just start.

- Have a thought? ... write it down.

- Have a thought? ... Ask a question.

- Have a thought? ... Make a phone call.

- Have a thought? ... Act on it.

- Have a thought? ... Action ...

Notice a pattern forming here?

Take what's in your head, throw it into reality by strapping a jet pack to it, and go. There comes a time when the planning must stop and the doing must start. Filter through the random nonsense, pick a thought, wind it up, let it go, and then follow it to where it leads you.

To weed through the random nonsense; after you write down a bunch of thoughts, let them marinate for a while to see if they take root. A few hours or days later, if you re-read your ever-expanding list ... most of the time, the nonsense will blow off in the wind, lose interest, and the ones that stick around ... put them in the action category.

~ Recap ~

- Indecision is a bad habit.

- Bad habits can be replaced with better habits.

- Work out a routine when a thought presents itself.

- Turn thoughts into actions.

Example:
Thought ... 3 ... 2 ... 1 ... Action!

Finding The Sweet Spot

Navigating the Spectrum

Whether you're in a relationship that is one day old or fifty years deep, everything you say and do will either affect that relationship positively or negatively; draw you closer together or repel you further away.

When you are aware of the potential effects you have on another individual who also just wants to live, love, be happy, and make the best out of this life, you can turn everything back onto yourself as if what they say or do to you has the same impact. Every word you say to them can be carefully constructed as a reflection of what words you would like them to say to you.

Even the painful truths you recognize in others can be spoken out of love and concern rather than hurtful jabs or condescending remarks. Truth, as harsh as it can be sometimes, can still deliver a healing message if presented from a caring heart of concern, but that same truth delivered on the tip of a derogatory poisonous dart will render a completely different outcome.

So ... Where is the Sweet Spot?

Before we go there, to uncover the underlying behaviors that veer from that sweet spot between too soft and too harsh, most attention needs to be focused on what I believe to be the biggest contributor in this battle for relational bliss, and that's the camouflaged killer called insecurity.

Insecurity can present itself in one of two different directions, with numerous variations in either direction. Once it's established, you'll know what to look for to make corrections in your relationships.

1. **Under-Compensation**
   ~ Usually displayed as mild to extreme shyness, low, or no self-esteem, or low to no confidence.
   ~ Most of the time, being the people pleasers that subconsciously believe their opinion doesn't matter, go with the flow or follow what everyone else is saying or doing just to fit in.
   ~ They pick a person or a crowd they think they would like to be like, based on their delusional version of what they believe it means to be self-confident.

   This unhealthy portrayal of self-confidence leads to the second direction.

2. **Over-Compensation**
   ~ Usually displayed as, in your face, belligerent, arrogant, self-righteous, better than everyone else attitude.
   ~ The person who tries to make those around them feel lesser so they can feel better about themselves.
   ~ Emphasizing everyone else's faults to take the attention off their own and most of the time, it's mistaken for and deceptively self-defined as being confident, strong, and independent.

Both are extreme versions of the spectrum of insecurity that vary to the center "sweet spot" of true security.

Sometimes those in the under-compensation category that's had enough of being taken advantage of, will realize their situation and want to correct it, but overshoot the target of true self-confident security, flip the switch, and catapult themselves into the over-compensation category.

Being taken advantage of is a real thing but, to an extent. in the under-compensation category, it's pretty much their own unrealized fault. They can't or don't stick up for themselves because they are too worried about stepping over an unrealistic boundary they've put on others' feelings. Because they are laser-focused on their feelings, they believe they can't disrupt the apple cart in anyone else's life because they risk being offended or being exposed for their inability to respond quickly with the best retort. They usually beat themselves up later for not saying what they wanted to, after they had a chance to think about it.

Those who over-compensate, couldn't care less about anyone's feelings, they just blurt out whatever comes to mind without any regard for consequence. They are also laser-focused on their feelings but in a selfish way. They are only concerned about protecting their feelings without transferring them to anyone else; while under-compensation is concerned about everyone else's feelings.

Mostly, they are inadvertently taught to be insecure in either direction by upbringing. On the one hand, if you don't know you're insecure in one or the other category, you don't have the tools necessary to make any lasting changes in the true, secure direction.

As I mentioned earlier about endless variations, also, don't be deceived into believing that because you don't possess every example in either category, you still don't fall into one. The first step toward true security is being aware of the fact that you fit into one or the other category, to varying degrees, and then being brutally honest with yourself by admitting that fact. Take the necessary steps forward toward perpetual personal development in the most productive ways possible.

Now that's on the table ...
what and where is the "sweet spot?"

The Sweet Spot!

That place where you can live in complete confidence and not worry about what anyone thinks or says about you. Your mood is unaffected by adverse circumstances or situations, stable-minded, and able to separate your emotions and feelings from the people, places, and things in your everyday life. To make the best, most positive, productive choices possible from now on to live the life you desire.

YEAH RIGHT!!! IN A PERFECT WORLD!!!

I know what you're thinking ... "You're completely overflowing the top of a taco bowl with a fresh pile of yester-lunch!" Although, yes, it's impossible to achieve an absolute state of perpetual nirvana, there is a way to live and maintain a better life if you have a solid anchor point target to focus on; to regulate yourself toward that target when things are going off track.

You certainly wouldn't model yourself after the worst things possible to improve your life ~ you shoot for perfection to improve yourself. You'll never achieve it this side of the grave, but if you don't aim for it, you'll never even get into the boat ... continuing to swirl around in the cesspool eddy of life, while simultaneously complaining about why you don't ever make it out of the harbor.

Let's break down a few bite-size pieces to shoot for, so we can get closer to the target.

- Be aware of which insecure category you tend to fall into the most.

- Be brutally honest with yourself by pointing out the behaviors you recognize keeping you from the sweet spot.

- Self-regulate towards equilibrium while you're shooting for the target.

   Not under or over-compensating for your insecurities.

   Stay in a state of self-awareness for each category.

   Re-calibrate your focus on a regular schedule towards

the sweet spot.

- When you "feel" like quitting ... Don't!

- If you do quit ... Start back up again!

- Introduce this concept to someone else so you can both be accountable to each other.

- If you're one of those perfectionist overthinkers;

  - When you mess up, forgive yourself, then continue without beating yourself up about it. It's ok to make mistakes.

  - You're no better or worse than anyone else.

- Enjoy the journey and don't forget to live life in the process.

Each has its challenges in the form of practice. No one is born with every skill necessary to survive this life. You must develop the ones you lack and eliminate those that harm you.

Under-compensation has to work at climbing out of their shell and practice being more assertive without over-shooting the target. Work at saying what they must say with firm confidence in their message while maintaining their skills to consider others' feelings. They also need to step over their unrealistic or non-existent boundaries by thinking they must be nice to everyone. They must also develop and protect healthy boundaries to stand up for themselves when others aren't nice to them.

**YOU teach people how to treat you
by either letting them walk all over you
or demanding they treat you with respect.**

Over-compensation has to dial things back and practice recognizing that other people have feelings as well. Respect their boundaries as you demand respect for yours. Stop believing that what they have to say is more important than those they're speaking with by interrupting them mid-sentence in what they are already saying. Recognize that when they are putting others down or calling them some derogatory name, they're doing so to boost their ego to feel better about themselves.

These behaviors must first be recognized in each category and confessed as an issue in themselves, otherwise, they will never move past those insecurities, staying stuck swirling in and out of the cesspool eddy until the pattern is broken.

Remind yourself every day if you must, but keep in mind that everything you do to improve yourself will automatically improve every one of your relationships. It all starts with self-awareness and admitting your flaws ... [**and yes, you have them in abundance**] ... it's the only way to continue moving forward toward healing.

You can not fix what you believe is not broken.

Mental Death by Observation

Tragically Conditioned Behaviors

Are you authentically you or a perverted version habitually passed down from generation to generation?

We've all been conditioned, to some degree, to believe that there are such things as good and bad when they are just words that we apply meaning to, and then place them on a spectrum of preferences.

For example;

Things we don't prefer to happen to us we call bad and the things we do prefer to happen to us we call good.

Now before you pick up some word stones to verbally pummel me with arguments of how murder, rape, theft, and any other horrible acts of human corruption are all "bad" things ... I'll say you would be right, so allow me to clarify this concept.

There are such categories as good and bad in cases of actions on this spectrum of preferences ... but ... if you trace back a "bad" action, they are always trained behaviors by a lack of understanding of the original divine design for humanity.

The more that original design fades further away from the pure source of truth, the more proper training also fades. Passing down with it, generational tainted and negative behavior patterns delivered specifically by the vehicle of observation.

So technically ~ yes ~ by a published definition, there are bad things ... but for all intents and purposes ... they all have one thing in common.

You can't undo what has already been done.

By no means is this to be cold or to downplay the acts themselves as not being definitionally bad things ... it's more of a factual reality in that it did already happen ... so now, what's the quickest way to recover from these events moving forward?

Of course, there is a natural progression of shock, anger, grief, acceptance, and recovery to go through, but there is a time that one needs to come to, that will be their turning point in moving forward ... and that is acceptance.

Acceptance opens the door to recovery.

If you notice ... every stage before acceptance keeps us in either a state of denial or victimhood making recovery next to impossible. The quicker you get to the acceptance part, the quicker you can recover. When you realize and embrace the reality ... "It is what it is" ... Or ... It happened, now What? Then you can start to move forward, regardless of, but still knowing what happened doesn't make it any less wrong.

The point would be that labeling events as "bad" things, usually keeps us locked in a holding pattern of anger, regret, resentment, and so on, staying in the mentality of "victim," and rehashing the events over and over again keeping us locked in the "past" prison.

Again, not downplaying the event itself, and yes, you may have been the actual victim of a physical tragedy, but owning the mental state of victimhood status as being a part of you will only keep you in a negative atmosphere of despair which only leads deeper into despair.

This is exactly what I'm trying to prevent.

Getting back on track with the original point of labeling circumstances as good or bad, but focusing on the bad label: Claiming something to be bad, also triggers other emotional spectrums of habitual, reactionary behaviors, so throughout the day we subconsciously experience a roller coaster of negative and positive feelings that toss us back and forth like waves crashing on the beach.

This is good ... that's bad ... those are good ... they're bad ...

If we're prone to choose negativity, the good things usually just slip through the cracks and aren't even noticed. While labeling something as bad, from a negative standpoint, automatically shows up on the radar as an abundant offender. It just comes naturally, so the "bad label triggers" set off a chain reaction of negative feelings and emotions that accompany the behavior, even though the circumstance and the reaction to that circumstance are two completely separate entities. (this alone is another separate topic)

A more stable way to look at your ever-changing circumstances is first to be aware of this behavior, then resist the need to categorize your emotional preferences into either "good" or "bad", but rather accept things as ... *"IT JUST IS" ~ "IT HAPPENED, NOW WHAT?"* ... then intentionally respond to every event in your life with the most productive and positive choices possible.

Once you establish this habit instead, you will develop a healthy mental attitude, so you can get on about your day without feeling the need to kick the cat or break something.
Try to practice recognizing destructive behaviors and emotions such as fear, worry, hate, unforgiveness, anxiety, stress, anger, control, etc. (all negativity). Then focus on replacing them with ones that build on constructive patterns like love, peace, gratitude, joy, patience, understanding, forgiveness, and so on (all positivity).

Waking Up From this Matrix.

There is an ultimate source of life, as mentioned above, which sustains life and embodies everything good, right, and positive in its most unadulterated form of perfection. The furthest you can move away from that source is a complete depletion of that source, or the ultimate form of perversion on the opposite side of that spectrum, bad, wrong, and negative.

You might be thinking, *"I thought you said not to see things as either good or bad."* ... Yes, I did, but, again, not definitionally, but rather in an attitude or a reactionary sense.

On the perversion side, is the explanation word that we reference as ultimate bad or evil. So to remain in a positive state of existence, we must strive towards the side of the spectrum that promotes the fullest life possible, the source of pure goodness.

Break it down.

So the chain of events that happen from thoughts to actions, from the standpoint of improper training or upbringing is ... something happens that we don't prefer ... we immediately (habitually) think that this "something" is a bad thing ... again, habitually, reacting to that belief because that's what we experienced growing up.

Those thoughts, actions, reactions, and behavior patterns are also attached to feelings and emotions that automatically surface as even more familiar territory, which root themselves as *"just being a part of you"*, or *"that is just the way I am,"* mentality. Registering that the circumstance was a bad thing ... while the same old negative, thoughts, reactions, and emotions have followed suit, you are now in a bad mood that you have just accepted as your hereditary and uncontrollable behavior loop.

All this happens in a split second because the habits are ingrained into one seamless state of existence. This chain of behaviors can be broken and starts with an awareness that this is happening inside of you.

What to do from here forward?

Take responsibility and accept that you can separate your automatic reactions and turn them into intentional responses by way of a personal choice.

Reactions are automatic;

Any "bad" reactions ... stress, worry, fear, anxiety, anger, offense, dread, despair, hate, unforgiveness, and anything else that stems from anything negative, wrong, or evil, are all just bad habits that can be "kicked".

Responses are intentional;

Replace with "good" responses ... love, peace, joy, contentment, acceptance, excitement, understanding, forgiveness, and anything else that stems from positive, right, and good. These can be developed into good habits.

This process is not going to be easy or an overnight occurrence. It has taken years to create these habits (some our whole lives) so it will take a while to reverse the process, but it will happen if you are determined and consistent.

Attitude is everything ... start right out of the gate with;

- I will go into this with the attitude of, *"I WILL do this UNTIL it works."*

- Stay completely away from the attitude of, *"I'll give it a TRY to see IF it works."*

If you choose the second attitude, you have already lost. This isn't something that some people have and others don't ... You always have the power to change! Your success is a promise as long as you don't quit ... yes, you will want to quit at times because you don't see anything happening in the beginning, but as the saying goes; *"Old habits are hard to die."*

Don't do this alone. Make sure you are accountable to someone ... never quit ... and you will experience one victory at a time.

T.D.H.D

Think ~ Declare ~ Honor ~ Do

Dealing with ADHD, Attention Deficit Hyperactivity Disorder? According to the Mayo Clinic, the key character traits of someone with ADHD are inattention, hyperactivity, and impulsivity. Symptoms include; trouble paying attention or staying focused and being easily distracted, careless mistakes, appearing not to listen, difficulty following through, avoiding, forgetting, or dis-liking tasks, losing items, fidgeting, being in constant motion, talking too much, interrupting, difficulty waiting and so on down the line.

I have been guilty of many, if not all, of the above-mentioned traits at one time or another, but have learned to work around most of them by first becoming aware and then finding ways of eliminating or at least managing most of them.

Keep in mind that a lot of those behaviors are just normal and don't need any diagnoses or medications to combat. By no means am I promising any cures to those who have been professionally diagnosed with this disorder.

My concern is that once a child is "diagnosed" by a so-called professional, they take on that stigma and wear it like a tattoo, something they can never get rid of, or be a slave to the pharmaceutical industry as a perpetual customer.

Again, I'm not a physician and am not suggesting that I have a cure or can diagnose your situation. I am just relaying to you the process I go through to shed light on my thinking and actions that I take to cope with challenges. The major challenge I face is focus and focus can be greatly enhanced by interest, because if you're not interested in doing what you're doing, then not only does focus fly out the window, it finds the nearest swamp to drown itself in.

To that, I would like to introduce to you my very own personal acronym, TDHD, and the counter routines I have used to develop my habits.

T. D. H. D.
Think - Declare - Honor - Do

This represents the unit of execution, as a whole, and I've structured my life like a business and compare each part of my being to a hierarchy. Business and entrepreneurship have always been an interest of mine, so you may have to model something different, but here it is, as I see it:

The Brain
This is your executive office, where your theories, techniques, ideas, conceptualizations, and beliefs swim around in the penthouse pool, smoking expensive cigars and sipping on little drinks with skewered olives. They're all locked inside with no keys and no way of escaping.

The Body
This is your factory, warehouse, employees, inventory, and

machinery: The means necessary to take a thought that comes down from corporate to produce enough power and turn it into an action.

The Arms and Legs

This is your transportation fleet that combines the instructions and the power necessary to transfer them into constructing, acting, applying, making, building, going, and doing.

Altogether as a whole unit and in conjunction with the sensory organs, we can accomplish whatever the imagination can come up with. That is IF every individual part of the whole is in harmony with each other and functions as one complete and well-oiled machine.

Going back to the opening acronym T.D.H.D.

The first three are all stuck in the office mulling things around, drawing diagrams, slamming gavels, and barking orders. CEO ~ (THOUGHT), its secretary ~ (DECLARATION), and the board ~ (HONOR) are all continuously sending signals down to the plant manager to start production, repair the machinery, or ship out inventory. If the transportation department ~ (DO) doesn't fire up the fleet and get things moving, nobody gets paid.

The BRIDGE between where you're at and where you want to be, and what you want and getting it is ACTION!

That could be business, leisure, or relationships ... in all areas and on all levels.

For the best possible action to be implemented, you must put legs and arms (your transportation, delivery fleet) to whatever has your interest and do it with your most productive abilities, have it be morally right, ethical, and legal. Have it be the most advantageous for you as well as everyone involved, and with the best attitude you can muster.

Drilling down further, dissecting each part of the process.

Think

The thought process. It doesn't matter whether your mind wanders or is focused, your creative thoughts trigger curiosity. From curiosity, you generate ideas, intuitions, creations, epiphanies, or revelations. This could be in life, business, relationships, etc. Determine whether it's worthy of your time and assign a task to your creations.

Then;

Declare

Boldly verbalize what you would like to do/accomplish. First to yourself, then to friends, colleagues, family, and business partners. This is MY idea! I will carry through until the end! I will make a game plan and take the first step! I will ask for help, search for wisdom, and learn what I need to do!

Then;

Honor

Hold yourself accountable. Make a solid commitment from your declaration!

Pin a finish date to your goal! Tell a partner, friend, colleague, etc. to hold you accountable also! Evaluate your target at specific checkpoints that you've set along the way!

Notice that the three above are still stuck in the head and don't do anything. The next one is when you jump feet first onto the field and start actually playing the game instead of just being a spectator, one of those armchair quarterbacks that have all the answers to win the game by screaming at the T.V. They also don't put down the popcorn bowl and beer can long enough to participate in making any kind of difference inside reality.

Then;

Do

Get the ball of thought rolling to create momentum. Turn your idea ... declaration ... and honor ... into a reality! Ask questions to seek answers for what you don't know! Tangible action starts building skin around the skeleton! Utilize every possible asset - all of your available nouns! Daily, weekly, monthly, and yearly goals to hit! Anything you can do that will bring "it" to fruition! Do it!!!

Rinse and repeat!

This is meant to be a process of turning your procrastination or inattention (focus) into a routine that will create better habits so your mind will no longer be your enemy but your ally.

Why Do We Give Up?

What To Do About It

We try something inside of our low levels of self-esteem. When we have low self-esteem, we don't try most things to the fullest of our abilities. We go into it with an attitude of: "I'll TRY it to see IF it will work" and not with the attitude of: "I WILL do it UNTIL it does work."

Past shreds of evidence have shown us failure equals pain, and nobody likes pain, so we build up this front by putting on some kind of role-play routine.

- The tough guy.

- The sad loser.

- The defeated victim.

- The downtrodden, "everything always" happens to me.

- The sympathy seeker.

This only covers up our damaged little inner selves with a protective shell, so we don't have to feel that pain.

Our efforts are always half of what they should/could be, and because you don't want to feel the pain of failure, you only go so far. When you see something not working, that's enough evidence for you to quit and tell everybody that it didn't work. Then you convince yourself that it's 100% true for your conscience to function. All the while sold on the "self-proclaimed fact" that your efforts were enough to lead you into eminent failure.

Your inner subconscious questioning to justify this behavior is; It's just going to fail anyway, so why try? Or, what's the point? Using blanket stereotype statements like; "Nobody", "Everybody", "Always", and "Never." All to justify why you should quit ... to get people to feel sorry for you. The sympathy seeker. This is all happening subconsciously behind the scenes and is necessary to pull out into the light to process.

It's a victim mentality that keeps you in a failure loop through a "**Self-Fulfilling Prophecy**." You gather evidence by what's known as "**Confirmation Bias**." Keeping you stuck in what's called "**Willful Ignorance**".

1. **Self-Fulfilling Prophecy;**
   When you confirm your false expectations with evidence that you're already hyper-focused on finding.
   You have found what you are determined to find, with nothing else being a possibility.

2. **Confirmation Bias;**
   Piggy-backs on Self-Fulfilling Prophecies, by ONLY finding the conclusions that you have already convinced yourself of finding.
   Not leaving any room for any other conclusions.

3. **Willful Ignorance;**
   This is a state of mind existence that you live in because

you can't see anything outside of what you have already convinced yourself of.

A habitual result of the first two perpetual processes to find what you have preconditioned yourself to find.

This is what's keeping you from full success because pain creates fear, fear creates hesitance, stacked hesitance creates procrastination and, as a result, nothing gets done (stagnation). So your underlined, beneath-the-surface issue is fear. So let's take it a step further and pull back the curtain of fear.

Fear is frequently a buildup of an exceedingly active imagination, subconsciously making the worst out of situations, blowing things out of proportion, or convincing yourself that things are much worse than they are.

Ok, so what can we do to reconcile this matter?

Past pains cause fear, fear causes hesitation, hesitation causes procrastination, and procrastination causes stagnation. So, let's trace it back to its origins to see what's happening beneath the surface. Starting with when you catch yourself in a moment of procrastination;

PROCRASTINATION

Tear it down piece by piece until you have entered the cave of the unknown (fear), and drag your monster (overreactive imagination) into the light (truth) to see what you're dealing with. Accept it for what it is. Put a bit in its mouth and start being the one leading "IT" around instead of "IT" leading you around. Nine times out of ten, whatever fear that's keeping you stuck is nothing more than a tiny harmless bug projecting its shadow against the wall of your imagination to give you the illusion that it's much bigger than it is.

Some examples would be:

Avoiding a conversation because you "think" it will end badly when the chances are 50/50 that it will end well. The negative side of your imagination is dominant, so you immediately assume the worst. Start conditioning your mind to catch yourself and "think" the best from now on.

If you're afraid to spend a few extra dollars because you "think" you'll run out of money. This comes from the mind frame of lack, excessive worry, or a poverty mindset. Start catching yourself and start reconditioning your mind frame for abundance, ... more is coming.

The same mindset that complains about every bill that comes in until the deadline hits but still begrudgingly pays it, nevertheless. ... Just willingly pay it when it comes in, without complaining, without hesitation. You have to pay for it anyway. Why not save yourself the upset and a negative emotional experience? Don't waste your energy on worthless emotions that change nothing.

HESITATION

What are my stacked hesitations that are causing procrastination? Not enough time. Not enough money. Not good enough. Not strong enough. Not tall enough. Whatever "thing" you are using as a hesitation to not move forward?

FEAR

What are the fears that are triggering those hesitations?

Are those fears real, or am I projecting a past failure? Something triggered pain in this situation and you're not seeing it as a completely separate and unique experience? How have I been subconsciously programmed to react because of those fears? What did I watch my parents do? How did they respond to situations like this? Am I copycatting their behavior?

PAIN

What have I experienced in the past that has caused this familiar pain?

Identify any pain and reconcile or make peace with each one. Always reconcile with your worst-case scenario and everything else in between won't matter. Recognize that it's real. It happened. You can no longer change that fact. Accept it for what it is.

Now what? What can I do from this moment forward to put it behind me? Realize that it has nothing to do with this situation. It's a new opportunity to change my future. It's a separate, unique opportunity to move forward. Make a new habit by saying, "It happened; Now what? Then choose the most productive and positive choice possible at that moment, tweaking things along the way when better choices present themselves.

Once you see it for what it is ... how your past pains caused your fears, causing hesitation, causing procrastination ... now you can do something about it instead of it crippling you into stagnation. Step on it, step over it, saddle it up, make friends with it, put it out of your mind altogether, but do whatever you have to do to move past it. Now you know what it is ... set it free!

This also means you have to get out of the habit of making excuses and start being mercilessly honest with yourself.

Excuses mean that you've been locked in a pattern of victim thinking, that "IT" is always the fault of something or someone else, and that "IT" is powerless to change. "IT" = Whatever you blame all your problems on ... why you're oppressed ... why you can't change ... why you're stuck where you're at ... whatever person/s, places, or things you default to ... what you have convinced yourself of through the "Self-Fulfilling Prophecy" ~ "Conformation Bias" ~ and "Willful Ignorance" cycle.

When you're honest with yourself and admit that you could be mistaken and probably are on numerous levels, you'll see many more doors open to you in the form of healing. This will, now, trigger a positive upswing of emotions instead of a negative downward spiral, as above.

You'll find that by implementing this information, once you're on this pathway, other things will present themselves to keep moving in the same direction to recovery.

Take the first step and the next will appear.

Try And Fail Or Do And Succeed

One Word Can Change Your Life

Your chances of success are exponentially increased with a one-word exchange.

Regarding our personalities, as much as we would all like to believe that we are what we are when we behave the way we do, it boils down to two things: Your outlook and the attitude you choose to display about the events that unfold. It has nothing to do with the actual circumstances that may arise.

I know full well how the everyday pounding of the circumstantial waves of life can drive you to believe that life is all about the sufferings, much less any purpose for it all. There's a little secret that, if or when you find it, will set you on a different path, both inside and out.

Have you ever stopped to wonder why something identical can happen in two separate lives and have two completely different responses? One is negative, and the other is positive.

If you ponder that fact alone, you can't help but conclude that it isn't the circumstance, because that was identical. It has to be the way someone chooses to respond to any given event because that is the only difference.

Some will argue that *"that's just the way I am,"* but your reactions can never define you as a person. It's a habitual reaction to a learned behavior because of watching someone else perform the same behavior, such as upbringing by parents or a heavy influence by teachers, other family members, peers, etc. However, like anything that can be learned by a desire to do so, something that was inadvertently taught as a negative behavior can also be un-taught and then re-taught to properly function within the guidelines of a positive healthy behavior pattern.

Each new day brings fresh ideas, opportunities, choices, and a drive to become better than you were yesterday. As crazy as it is, it only boils down to the way YOU CHOOSE to respond to anything life gives you daily.

It might take a little time, depending on how rooted you are in your behavior patterns, but you CAN strive to change into the positive person you could be if you set your mind like bedrock and discard the word TRY and replace it with DO. Putting action to anything, with a strong desire and emotion, repeated enough times will generate new habits, producing new results and eventually a new lifestyle. In essence, a new personality.

You rarely succeed at anything if you TRY, but your chances of success increase exponentially if you set out to DO instead.

~Try~

Try, is just a half-hearted attempt to prove yourself wrong because it's a disbelief in your abilities (your insecurities) that sabotages your confidence, causing you to fail most of the time.

If your self-talk sounds something like this ... *"I'll TRY it to see ~IF~ it will work."* Think about this ... The word IF lives in a hypothetical environment and should only be pondered in a situation. It should never be an excuse not to do something.

~Do~

Do is more of a wholehearted commitment to see a goal, a dream, or an idea through to its completion, UNTIL you succeed at whatever you put your mind to.

If your self-talk sounds something like this ... *"I will DO it ~UNTIL~ it DOES work"* the word "UNTIL" lives in a projected evidential outcome with the belief of that environment becoming a reality, which defines faith.

When you eliminate the whole concept of "try" from your life, you can now work towards a goal that you know WILL succeed. It will take time and sometimes brief "opportunities", which some refer to as failures, that will add to your knowledge for later on in life.

Set your face like a flint and start DOING!

The actual difference between try and do is the attitude. If you start something with the attitude of, *"I'll try it to see IF it will work,*" there isn't any motivation to start with, so you'll lose interest if there's even the slightest opposition that arises.

~But~

If you start something with the attitude of, *"I will do it until it DOES work,"* you start with a massive amount of motivation to catapult you off the starting line. This keeps you going even through adversities until your goal is reached, in addition to striving to find something new to further your goals.

~ Try ~
Seeks opportunities to quit!

~ Do ~
Seeks opportunities to succeed!

YOUR ATTITUDE IS EVERYTHING!

Is There Any Purpose to Your Depth of Suffering?

It's Not The Suffering ~ It's What It Does

If there's no purpose to what you endure, your life's a worthless drowning of empty motions.

The age-old question or ponderings of meaning for the purpose inside the box of suffering have always been a topic of discussion, either in professional circles or just sitting around a campfire with those who commiserate on a more personal level.

If your mind has never experienced constant, daily, crippling torment, there aren't any words to explain to someone how deep that goes, but the deeper the torment goes, the deeper the connection and understanding go with levels that can't be reached by those who play on the surface.

The less you suffer on any level, the less you can relate to those who have. This means that if you've had a perfectly padded life unaffected by the sufferings that most of the population has experienced, you can't have a very deep conversation with that majority either.

To say that suffering is a good thing might not be far off the mark, but ... wishing suffering on someone depends on what outcome you desire for them.

- Wishing them harm and suffering for the sake of suffering just to be mean or vindictive isn't a good thing.

- But, wishing them to endure suffering so they can get past what is now keeping them in a state of perpetual misery, learn what they need to learn, and get to the other side of it as a better person. This will give them more understanding and a depth of life that can't be achieved if they don't go through it, which is a good thing.

There is purpose in pain and suffering.

You must go through a certain progression to get to the other side of anything in life.

- No one likes to go to school (although there are a few), but the result is a useful education.

- Nobody likes exhaustingly difficult, hard labor, but the result is the tangible product of that labor.

The same with pain and suffering. As the subtitle suggests, if there's no purpose to what you endure, your life's a worthless drowning of empty motions.

I will try to lay out the progression from start to finish in the process and how the result creates the purpose; that is if you're patient enough to follow it to its fruition.

The more you suffer, the more you think … The more you think, the more you contemplate … The more you contemplate, the more you search for answers … The more you search for answers, the more you discover ... The more you discover, the more you learn ... The more you learn, the more wisdom you gain ... The more wisdom you gain, the more you're capable of connecting on a deeper level ... The more you're capable of connecting on a deeper level, the more you're able to lead others through suffering ... The more you lead, the more you bring into the freedom of a deeper connection; and that, I believe, is the purpose of life itself. To connect on the deepest level possible ... and the cycle continues.

I should point out that the list above can take a turn in either direction at each juncture for the best or worst, depending on what your attitude is when you get there.

In the first stage when you suffer, and you will, you can think that your suffering is worthless and end up learning nothing. This will send you around the same mountain over and over again and in the same sufferings ... or you can think about what happened and what you need to learn so you can move to the next phase. Each phase is another step in the process to bring you to a deeper connection.

- Who wouldn't want the deepest connections possible?

- The deepest sufferings render the deepest connections.

- Don't throw away your suffering by complaining.

- Learn what it's teaching to become a better YOU!

Worthless Emotional Energy

Time To Clean House

If there's a broken or worn-out item in your house that is to the point of being unfixable or worthless, what do you do next? You throw it away or dispose of it, of course. But what would happen if you kept all of those things that were broken and worn out beyond repair?

They would pile up and clutter the working space around you, slow you down, inconvenience you by getting in your way, increase the load, bog things down, and cause a negative unnecessary source of frustration.

So what would be the logical thing to do in this case?

Pick out all of those sources of frustration and eliminate them from your existence. Correct?

Seemingly unrelated ... but I would like to experiment.

Follow me on this one.

If I took a pencil and held it straight out in the air and told a crowd full of people that I would count to 3 and open my fingers, giving them full advance knowledge that I was going to do this. I then told everybody to collectively, and with every cell in their body, as hard as they possibly could, to worry about the pencil NOT hitting the ground.

Based on the laws of nature, specifically gravity, what would the outcome be?

Everybody knows that the law of gravity would prevail every time you tried to test it, so the obvious conclusion would be to render ahead of time the pointless attempts to even think about worrying about it, much less doing it.

Think about worrying for a minute and ask yourself some questions.

- Has there ever been a time in history that worry changed anything from happening or not happening?

- Has worry ever helped anyone achieve anything or made anything better?

Don't confuse worry for concern, and don't deceive yourself into believing that you're concerned when you are actually worrying.

~ **Worry** ~

Worry tries to change something by doing nothing but stressing over something that can not be changed or concentrating negative energy toward a circumstance, event, person, etc. because they want to control the outcome that's out of their control.

~ **Concern** ~

Concern takes necessary action steps and does what it can to change the course of an unpreferred outcome without working itself up over unchangeable outcomes. Concern accepts things for what they are and productively adapts to changes.

Do we then assume that we can render worry a broken, worn-out, worthless emotion and safely eliminate it from our emotional backpack, ultimately loosening our emotional load?

I believe, subconsciously, we all know that worry doesn't do any good, so why do we still do it?

Since there is such a thing as choice ... and with choices available on every part of a spectrum, there has to be a perfect rendition and a perverted rendition of the same emotion.

If we trace negativity, bad feelings, discomfort, or discontentment back to its source, we will find an emotion that is, in essence, the perverted version of the originally intended pure emotional choice that the Source of all life has instructed us to live by: The one that not only predicts but promotes and produces life.

The unfortunate part of the full spectrum of choice is the unintended side of the spectrum: The one that not only predicts but promotes and produces death.

Of course, it doesn't show that in the brochure, and as a matter of fact, its deceptive marketing tactics come in the form of selfishness ~ driven by the stubborn side of our ego called the flesh. Where we think that the happiness we seek comes from material possessions, open relationships, big houses, endless money, fancy cars, and the like.

Worry is an absence of trust.

If we don't trust that the Source of life has everything under control, we inadvertently believe that everything is up to us, which is mistrust. If everything is up to us, the only thing in our control from that point on is our emotions. If you choose the perverted side of trust, the consequence is a worthless emotion that, compared to the broken and worn-out items in your house, will pile up and clutter the working space in your mind. It will also slow you down, inconvenience you by getting in your way, increase the load, bog things down, and cause a negative unnecessary source of frustration.

By using this same logic, how many other emotions can you think of that produce the same effects?

Comparing the house story above, what would be the logical conclusion to choose from, not only the broken physical items but the broken emotional items as well?

Pick out all sources of frustration and work to eliminate them from your existence. Not in the unrealistic sense that you will never experience any negative or bad thing ever again, but when you do, you will have the tools to combat those emotions as you are the controller and not the controlled.

For instance;

Immediately recognize when something breaks beyond repair to throw it away immediately. Don't even give it a chance to pile up.

Emotions have a purpose. Recognizing them for their intended purpose and adjusting accordingly will render a much better outcome.

Example;

Anger ... the negative side of anger starts as discontentment, unacceptance, and frustration, then it progressively gets worse and into bitterness, unforgiveness, and rage. If given to its full strength, ending in uncontrollable murderous violence.

The positive side and intended purpose of anger is a powerful motivator to change things for the better, like the quest to eliminate evil men who are bent on destruction; the ones that took selfishness and anger in the opposite direction. It starts the same but shifts into the intended positive, right, and good influence to direct that energy.

From this point forward, I challenge you to take every thought or action and mull over it first, before it just flies out as an uncontrollable habitual reaction. Think about the process from thought to action so you can maneuver a better, more positive, and productive outcome.

Choose the original designed purpose for each emotion, and distinguish what that is ... ask yourself if following through with it until it reaches its fullest potential renders a positive outcome or a negative one. Then you will have your answer.

The original design always renders the most positive, right, and the best outcome possible.

Strive for the top of that spectrum and you will do well in life.

I Should ~VS~ I Will

Should've ~ Would've ~ Could've ... never have and never will amount to anything tangible!

I SHOULD quit smoking, I SHOULD probably stop drinking so much, I SHOULD eat better, I SHOULD start exercising ... do all these statements sound painfully familiar? How about, "Hey old friend, we SHOULD get together sometime over coffee."

What do these statements have in common?

SHOULD ~ is an open-ended word that usually leads nowhere, unlike WILL. Will is a solid, more of a closed-ended statement that screams confidence and certainty.

SHOULD ~ is reserved for ballpark statements like, "I should be back by around 4:00." When there's no way to predict the exact future, but never used in the goal-setting arena.

With that in mind, as long as we're bringing up the word should, everything that comes out of your mouth needs to be a closed statement, as in, as soon as you say "I should quit ... or I should stop doing this or that ..." whatever "that" is ... stop and immediately replace it with a more solid statement.

You already know you SHOULD! ~ Make it a "WILL" statement! Put a time and date on it! ~ Then ... EXECUTE!

Replacing "I SHOULD do it" with "I WILL do it" ... and then immediately acting with the confidence of a 6-year-old with a Batman cape and skivvies combo ... WILL cause your life to change for the better whether you want it to or not.

But hopefully, you do.

Tell yourself out loud if you have to ... "I will stop smoking TODAY," ... "I will stop buying alcohol TODAY," ... "I will eat right TODAY," ... "I will exercise TODAY," ... and then just do it.

Fight through the cravings ... You are stronger than that!

Once you push through your weak moments a few times, it eventually turns into a habit. So instead of wasting your life, doom scrolling on social media or endless hours on video games, find something to replace it with, a better activity like reading a book or learning a new skill.

Make up your mind and do it.

Yes, it's going to be difficult, and yes, it's going to test you, seemingly beyond your limitations. Fight through it and do what you know to be right by replacing SHOULD with WILL and keep doing it until whatever you're doing is done.

YOU WILL BE GLAD YOU DID! ~ YOU ROCK!!!

NOW GET OUT THERE AND SADDLE SOME DRAGONS!

Oil Your Happy Hinge With Gratitude

Grateful = Happy

True happiness doesn't hinge on a circumstantial outcome but more on the attitude that you take inside that circumstance.

The words **Good** and **Bad** are terms based on our self-defined expectations of a personal preference or non-preference. Straight to the point, if you want to change your attitude ... change your expectational preferences.

A suggestion would be to abandon your presupposed judgments of how you think life should turn out based on the unrealistic expectations that it should always end the way you prefer. Remain open to everything happening the way it actually does.

In other words, get rid of the terms good and bad altogether, and now after every circumstance that happens, choose the best course of action forward by saying;

"It happened. Now what?"

Completely skip altogether the temptation of categorizing any situation or circumstance into the labels of either "Good", or "Bad".

It happened ... Now What? Then choose the best possible productive pathway forward.

Happiness, also, does not depend on anything going the way you want it to or getting what you want. It simply depends on the choice you make to be happy regardless of anything else.

I will try to word this as painlessly as possible, but if you're an unhappy miserable person ~ I would wager a considerable amount of potatoes that you're an ungrateful person as well.

Ungrateful = Unhappy

The two walk hand in hand and cleverly deceive you into believing, as the sand is still fresh in your toes, that happiness comes BEFORE gratefulness when, in fact, it's the contrary.

So here's the skinny ...

If your internal happiness is affected by your external circumstances ... then you're not truly happy! You're just skipping along the surface from preference to preference.

In that, the sad truth is the search for happiness is sometimes cloaked behind the drive for material possessions, leading those who choose to be deceived by that never-ending pursuit, empty and lacking in the intended outcome.

A true search for happiness is found inside each one of us placed there by the Creator of life itself, so what that means is ... you don't have to have money, houses, cars, relationships, fame, fortune, or any other external material possession to fully obtain and live a life in a contented state of peace, full of joy and happiness no matter where you are or what you have or don't have.

True lasting inner peace and happiness come from within ... what you already possess ... where you already live ... and who you are right now.

Let go of your preferential expectations and just live as the advertised garage sale items do ...

AS IS!

Interest Is The Gateway To Change

Lost Interest? ~or~ Became Familiar?

The power of "Interest" is an amazing force, because with it, you can concentrate intensely, endure almost anything, and live in a realm devoid of excuses!
But without interest, those same materials, circumstances, events, etc. will render a completely different outlook.

Such as;

"I don't have the time, money, energy, know-how" or every other excuse in the book to label whatever you're choosing as an alternative reason to do or keep doing what it is you're engaged in.

So before you make a subconscious assumption to veer away from any decision ... process it through critical thinking to arrive at the most educated conclusion possible. It just might be a lack of interest, which most times isn't a legitimate excuse for anything that proves helpful in your life.

If you are open to learning, you gain more knowledge, triggering more curiosity, which ultimately births interest. Once you're interested, you can do a tremendous amount more than what you think you're capable of. Suddenly ... you can come up with the time or find the money, face the fear, and conquer whatever you need to conquer ... and that is where you will find your motivation.

Instead of making mountains out of molehills ... Make molehills out of mountains.

If you're dissatisfied with your life, chances are you only know what you don't want, without its counterpart ... want ... in other words, you've lost some desire.

Not knowing what you want or where you want to go will subconsciously lock you into a state of perpetual dissatisfaction, unrest, and emptiness, and, most of the time, sink you into varying depths of depression.

Then you resort to the **WHY**ning ... WHY me, WHY now, WHY this .. but boarding the "**WHY**" train will keep you stuck at the station of complacency at its mildest forms and at its worst, the deeper dungeons of despair. So, before you quit your job or leave another relationship ...

Think about this ...

Losing interest is just becoming familiar with what was once curiosity and you can expect it will happen with the next job or relationship ... and the next one ... and the next, until you can take what you have now and find other ways of introducing different interests into it to keep the fire alive.

So, continue learning new things about whatever professional or personal relationship you're involved in right now.

Open new doors, create new outlooks, dig deeper into understanding on a deeper level, and mix up the routine, but don't think for a second that because you've lost interest in something, it's time to move on.

When you feel you're losing interest ... change your perspective to breathe new life into what you already have.

Stay curious friends.
Continue to choose love and understanding.

2
CONTROVERSIAL
OBSERVATIONS

SCIENCE ~ POLITICS ~ RELIGION ~ HUMOR ~ RANTINGS

—————⟫⟫◆⟪⟪—————

If you stand back and see things for what they are,

you'll notice patterns forming around you.

Sometimes the things you thought were real,

were nothing more than a dissipating smokescreen.

This section is a compilation of observations within organizations
that have weaved themselves into society and the inconsistencies
noticed by taking a few steps back and watching them play out
like a Hollywood screenplay.

Random Acts of Blindness

Politically Driven Nonsense

How bad does it have to get before people recognize the fabricated political and pseudo-science conditioning?

The Color Code

You CAN'T be any less of whatever color you were born with. You CAN be less deceived by politically driven nonsense that tells you to identify as a victim so they can manipulate you into groups to carry out their "divide and control" agenda.

Those who fall for the victim mentality are the easiest to control by getting them to fight against those who take responsibility for their own lives and fight for freedom. The deception is that those who believe they are fighting for freedom by advocating for a preferential political affiliation, are blinded by what they want to see instead of the truth right in front of them. Unfortunately, free handouts are extremely attractive to weak-minded victimhood mentalities who like to avoid responsibility.

If you rely on handouts, take action and make the necessary

changes to do what you have to do to stop relying on the government for your existence. Yes, sometimes people are "down on their luck" and need assistance as a stepping stone to bring them to the next phase in life but it's not meant to take advantage as a permanent form of lazy income.

If you want to break free from dependency on those who deceive you into believing you are entitled to receive handouts;

Stop listening to them when they try to convince you that you are powerless without them or are in any way a victim. This is a manipulative tactic to control you into being reliant on their handouts and, therefore, under their control. Once you realize that fact, it's up to you to be responsible enough to blaze your own path. Pay your own debts, earn your own keep, accept that whatever may have happened to you ... happened ... and now it's time to move forward without letting it define your future. Take your life and make it what you want it to be. Ask questions, learn new skills, start a side hustle ... find a way out of your seemingly hopeless situation.

Truth Is Not Negotiable!

So those who have any "control" over anyone, from the smallest individual to the largest groups, will, to some degree, try everything in their power to silence whatever "truth" that goes against their plans. So a gauge to determine where truth rests is to see where all the forced censorship is coming from and run in the other direction.

> **Side Note:** Dictatorship doesn't necessarily have to be someone who takes over countries. They can also be individuals in relationships.

<u>YOUR</u> Truth Isn't Necessarily <u>THE</u> Truth

Do you want to navigate to respectable places, make a difference, or feel good about yourself? Stop finding things to complain about or victim groups to identify with.

Take responsibility for the way you turned out, REGARDLESS of who had any influence on your outcome.

Stop feeling sorry for yourself and wallowing in self-pity. Start focusing on what you CAN do, or HAVE done, and things that DID work out.

EVERYTHING is a choice from this second forward! Everything that has happened from the last second backward no longer matters in your existence ~ except for lessons.

You are NOT a color, religion, sexual preference, job status, or belong to any ethnicity ... you are a member of one human race with differing characteristics, created to do great things ... it's up to you to make up your mind to do them ~ then put some actions behind that mindset and get it done.

Blind Affiliation

Those who have been sucked into a political affiliation with no positive action backing it.

This isn't a right vs. left bashing session; it's an educational side-by-side comparison of policies that are not working for the good of anyone involved. Both sides have strong points and weak points, both sides have over-the-top agendas that are only in place to control the population into believing it's the other side's fault that we're all in this mess.

Nobody is trying to get you to change your values or your passions, just your focus. Keep what works best for the greater good of everyone involved and scrap what doesn't. It should be that simple. Unfortunately, most are sold out to one side or the other because they only focus on a few positive points they believe about that party.

This is not against "Republican and Democrat" it's against Good and Evil. Stop letting the Evil convince you that you are against your neighbor. We all want to live in peace, enjoy our friends and families, and be free to love and be loved, regardless of what your political affiliation is.

There are people out there who are bent on destroying peace

because they have none. They are sociopaths without mercy or care for your way of life. They want total world domination and will stop at nothing to get it. Their overinflated ego is driven by arrogance, greed, and absolute selfishness.

AND IT IS NOT THE FRIENDS, FAMILY, OR NEIGHBORS THAT HAVE DIFFERENT POLITICAL VIEWS THAN YOU!!!

These lunatics are trying to turn us against each other so they can take advantage of the chaos. Stop bickering about who believes what. Your hatred towards people who have opposing political views is only feeding the flames of disunity.

This fight is much bigger than anybody who takes the office, whether you wear a mask or not. These are all smoke screens to skew your vision.

I could go on for days about this subject but the message is unity. Stop fighting against your fellow Americans because you don't believe in the same politics, this is nonsense.

Free Speech ~ For All

If you believe in free speech, but only when it benefits you ... then you don't believe in free speech, you believe in a dictatorship but you just happen to be on the same side as the dictator... and if you think the same way as the dictator, you agree with that dictator.

So then you have to ask yourself a sobering question ... How does that make you feel?

As the saying goes from the beginning of time ... there are always two sides to every story.

So If today you don't speak up against censorship because you agree with the ones censoring ... tomorrow, when they start to censor you, it will be too late.

Freedom of speech is not a preferentially convenient one-sided opinion. It's whatever anyone wishes to say, even if you don't want to hear it or it offends you.

Don't seek to eradicate others' opinions because they differ from yours. Learn to deal with it!

Hypocrisy At It's Best

If you preach intolerance, violence, division and bleed hatred for 4 years straight and then overnight start drooling on about unity, peace, love, and tolerance ... It's dumbfounding in a way, but understanding human nature and the way we all tend to cover our imperfections with the padded judgments of self-righteous intentions, I do see how this could be explainable to an extent.

However, It still always catches me off guard and makes me shake my head and wonder if they even believe what they're saying.

‑‑‑•‑◆‑•‑‑‑

Separation to Divide and Conquer

I love music, art, design, writing, and all other forms of creative outlets. If I share an interest with another artist, I will support them by purchasing an album, painting, or a book ... great job for accomplishing stuff; awesome. But what I could not give a flippin rippin fuzzy rats hairy underarm lint ball, is what color or gender they are.

I can't stand this new agenda to keep separating people's accomplishments by their exterior flesh color or what kind of private luggage they sport underneath their clothing.

‑‑‑•‑◆‑•‑‑‑

Deception turns my stomach...

Not just the deceivers but those who are being deceived.

Deceivers are driven by such hatred that they are blinded by their own derangement. All the while corruption has gotten so heinous in the political realm that it has turned good people against each other by polarizing them for power and selfish gain ... and by such petty nonsense items I might add.

They push to keep as many people divided as possible ... hijacking media outlets, educational institutions, and entire world views to throw off the scent of their stench. Inadvertently recruiting those who have been hooked by their bait of lies ... claims of caring for you to your face while ripping out the foundations of freedom one lie at a time.

For those who have swallowed the bait, my sincere hope is that something shakes your foundations enough to wake you from your slumbering existence in the matrix and cease to be their mouthpiece of destruction.

You would do well to drop any political attachment to either party, step back, and see things for what they are. Both "wings" belong to the same foul fowl.

Toxic Masculinity

Twisted Political Version

The misconception side of the modern movement of toxic masculinity is that the hierarchical structure of man is suppressing women, which is partly true, but that's only the case if the man is physically or mentally controlling.

The true, original structure for hierarchical humanity is the man being the leader or head of his family, the builder, protector, provider, conqueror, and natural-born warrior.

His job is to protect the physically weaker parties and everyone in his care as the protector and provider, not the controlling bully who barks out and commands what to do or not do. Unfortunately, when some men get into power, that power goes straight to their heads, no matter how small the position of power is.

They think they have to control everything ... as in, external control ... things outside of their ability to predict outcomes, but attempt to control them anyway.

True mature masculine control is being in control of your internal being, as in your thoughts, emotions, actions, reactions, and everything else you have total and absolute control over.

Trouble is, that many don't know how to control their inner emotional being because they were never taught how to.

So the true structure of the human hierarchy ... is the man at the top because it's his job to be the protector, conqueror, warrior, lover, provider, and king.

This position does not take away any importance, respect, or love from those in his care, such as women and children, which is the perfect structure of hierarchy for humanity.

The deceptive reality of leadership which veers toward mild to severe variations of a dictatorship mentality is sometimes mistaken for masculine leadership ... but couldn't be further from the truth.

Pro-Life / Pro-Choice

Issues in Both Courts

What is the difference between choice and life? I don't believe that it has to be a separate thing or something you have to make a solid line in the sand, as far as being on one side or the other... and that's it!

If you're pro-life, choosing life is, in essence, pro-choice and if you're pro-choice, a person's choice to live as they wish is pro-life.

It all boils down to a deeper understanding of each person's way they see the world, so let's throw this right out there;

Arguing your point of view and trying to selfishly force someone else to see things the way you see them ... never has and never will be an effective means of communication, so bantering back and forth about what you believe about this subject has never ... isn't now and never will be ... resolved by arguing your point in that manner.

The ONLY way to effectively communicate in any given situation is to see things through the eyes of those you oppose and understand why they believe the way they believe.

This DOES NOT mean that you AGREE with them!

It simply means that you can put yourself in their shoes long enough to understand why they believe the way they do ... That's it!

So how do we bridge the gap and fill in the understanding part without labeling it an agreement or disagreement?

First and foremost;
Get rid of your insatiable desire to be right.

This takes the pressure off of both parties to "win the argument" and makes it an intellectual conversation among grown adults who independently believe what they believe. From there, you can still walk away believing what you believe, but now without hostility attached to it, which is by far a more effective and superior way of communication.

Breaking it down into simple terms that everyone can grasp:

Pro-Life:

Those who choose to believe that a fertilized egg is an actual growing baby human being with a soul that deserves to be alive just as much as you choose to be alive now.

Pro-Choice:

Those who choose to believe that whatever is inside of a woman's body are lifeless tissues that aren't a human being or a living soul until it's outside of the body.

> Both sides have a belief system that drives them to act on that belief and do what they do because of that belief. Nothing more, nothing less ... Continuing forward.

Pro-Life:

Seeing it from the standpoint of believing it's a living soul, they see it comparatively as a baby who is already outside the body and under the parent's care.

That being the case, if a baby is outside the womb and the parent is beating that child or trying to cut it up, how many of you would stand there and watch them do it?

If you would do everything in your power to stop them from taking a human life ... someone from a pro-life point of view is trying to do the same thing, but shifting it back to when they believe life starts in the womb.

Pro-Choice:

Seeing it from the standpoint that, from the point of conception, it isn't a living soul, comparatively in most cases, it's nothing more than a part of the woman's body that can be discarded at will.

That being the case, if someone chooses to get a haircut and throw away the chopped-off hair, the view is ... what's the problem?

In the wake of Roe vs Wade ... or any other controversial topic in the news, for that matter, there is an eruption of emotions on both sides of the spectrum, either for or against whatever the hotbed of coals on the subject matter is.

You have differing opinions in every arena, be it the news outlets, social media, or every public space that offers a place to voice your beliefs to the world.

Most people agree with democracy as long as favor lands on their side of the fence but then have an enormous problem with it when a ruling isn't in their favor. They come up with multiple reasons why it's unconstitutional, unfair, unjustified, or a downright travesty of justice.

A pro-life victory and a pro-choice loss: Again, both are driven by their convictions based on a perception of labeling it as either a person or a thing.

Unfortunately, not everything comes in a cute little black and white package perfectly wrapped in a bow and on a solid yes or no line of decision. In most events, it's on a case-by-case basis that needs to be weighed on the scales of what's best for everyone involved, not just one point of view against the other.

For one ... nothing ever gets resolved in that way of thinking ... and two, it leaves many doors wide open to take full advantage of an inflexible system of cut-and-dried rules and regulations.

For instance:

If the law states that anyone can get an abortion anytime and anywhere ... then the responsibility of the individuals involved to think ahead about the possible consequences can be overlooked at the moment. If there is a pregnancy, they can use it, after the fact, as a form of birth control instead of choosing to be responsible from the start.

On the other side of the fence, if the law states that all abortions are illegal, then the consequences, in cases of self-inflicted abortions, will be more harmful than if they went into a fully equipped facility.

There are issues of life and death of the mother, some rape cases, and so on but those are very minimalistic cases in that area.

If you see things from multiple angles; say, if pro-life is the law at the time, the argument comes up that it's taking away the "rights" of the women involved, but if pro-choice is the law, another argument arises that now it's taking away the "rights" of the child involved. Nobody wins in this battle.

I've heard everything on social media platforms from being controlled by angry old white men to stripping away the rights of every woman everywhere and going back to the dark ages.

This goes through a process of, whoever is on the proverbial losing side. In either case, there are feelings of anger and resentment that let loose a flood of emotions because of the loss. Then eventually it regulates back into equilibrium when they find out things aren't as bad as everyone is making them out to be.

Either way, people will continue to believe what they believe in whatever direction they choose to believe it.

The point is this:

- Life will go on, (depending on where you place the point of life beginning)

- See things through others' eyes rather than forcing someone to see things through yours.

- Be flexible and see things for what they are and not always what you want them to be.

- Everyone has a point of view and some won't share yours.

- Love and understanding go a lot further than hate and judgment.

Hive Mind of (un)Social Media

Rantings About Hotbed Topics

The biggest problem with effective communication these days is that people think their personal opinions matter more than everybody else's, and because they believe it to be true ... that's enough evidence that it is true.

Opinions seem to have replaced the truth.

We all have worldviews and opinions ... we all have the potential to be wrong, but that pesky, selfish, egotistical thing called human nature doesn't like that very much, so we'll defend those worldviews and opinions to the death of perfectly good relationships.

A high percentage of every post I see on (un)social media, after every news flash, has to do with how someone can't stand how someone else is running their life and will rant and complain about how wrong THEY are, all the while thinking that what they are ranting about is supreme wisdom.

Pro-life against pro-choice, black against white, religious against atheist, republican against democrat, and whatever else you can use to separate yourself from another people group to prove to yourself that you're somehow better for thinking differently.

By doing so, you shove them into your insecure and self-righteous boxing ring to justify your verbal left hook.

> "How dare you not succumb to my point of view, you peasant?"

I'll let you in on another secret to maneuvering through this already strewn battlefield full of verbal landmines. We all have to try our best to navigate this life, to live it the best way we know how, and aside from a few bad apples, we all want to love and be loved, to live in a peaceful world full of happiness and contentment.

Everyone does what they do because they think it's the right thing to do ... Read that again! It all boils down to that, so if you could step back a few steps and consider that before your future attempts at tossing another victim under the non-stop charter bus to your throne room of judgment ... it would defuse many unnecessary rantings.

Before you toss your first word grenade over the social feed fence into someone else's post yard, and instead of assuming they are doing or saying something that vindictively pets your cat fur in the wrong direction, try genuinely asking them what they mean by what they say or do to see if you can't see things from their point of view. You just might be surprised at the outcome.

Do it out of concern and love for another human being, who

also lives and breathes the way you do, and ask yourself a few questions before you unleash the rant wolves.

1. Most importantly, ask yourself ... Could "I" be wrong?

   ◦ If that's possible, which it is ... ask the next question.

2. Could it be possible that they are doing or saying what they believe to be the right thing to do or say?

   ◦ If that's possible, which it is ... ask the next question.

3. Could I see things through their eyes to understand how they came to their conclusions?

   ◦ This does not mean you have to agree with them ... just understand them.

   ◦ Am I just attempting to be a self-imposed freedom fighter for my own opinions on how I see the world?

4. Would life continue if I didn't rant about what I believe?

   ◦ If so, heavily consider snipping the wires to your triggers and live the rest of the day knowing you have done your part in keeping the peace.

5. How can I be less judgmental and more understanding?

6. How can I be less hateful and more loving?

I could go on for the next week asking questions, but I'll leave the rest of those questions to you ... I don't want to do all the work here. Always put someone back together better than you found them ... and that includes yourself as well.

THE BLINDED EYES OF THOSE UNWILLING TO SEE

IT DOESN'T MATTER HOW LOUD YOU SCREAM TO THE DEAF

If you bottle up anything, eventually it will spill out of whatever container you are trying to keep it in ... and many are reaching the top of that container.

If you study behavioral psychology to any degree, you will uncover the deeper truths of why you think and do what you do. So when you notice a certain behavior or pattern either in yourself or others, you will immediately recognize mild to severe inconsistencies in those behaviors.

If you notice them in yourself, you can make some adjustments to course-correct the future "you". If you notice them in others, you can try to point things out that will get them to think about their decisions in life.

However ... if you notice an entire movement run by people in power and based on the negative immature side of human behavior, things get too irritating to sit back and not say anything. These irritations are mainly because of the injustices of indoctrination, deceptively entrenched in the progressive movement that is being force-fed to the populace through social media and mainstream news outlets.

Unfortunately, not everyone digs into the psyche, so they're taking advantage of ill-informed and weak-willed individuals to push a false narrative for the purpose of mass control.

Injecting a personal and political science into the bloodstream of humanity that is light-years away from real science, is producing nothing but mass confusion and polarization by the truckload.

Grown adults ... and by "adults" I'm speaking loosely and mean in the physical body only ... because the mental and spiritual sides of that human triad are grossly skewed by 'not taking into consideration that maturity goes much deeper than just ingesting physical food to keep you alive. You must "feed" all three tiers of human existence to be a complete, fully mature, adult.

Pointing out these people and their wicked agendas will, of course, cause some controversy because the ones who have already drank the Kool-Aid and swallowed the blue pill that locked them into the Matrix will inadvertently defend these lies out of that false sense of loyalty to "the cause" and the need to feel important ... another insecurity rooted in immaturity.

Looking at things from two separate angles, you naturally come to different conclusions.

On the one hand, these people in power that are sending others off the cliff of intellectual maturity are either deceived themselves and are just carrying the hoodwink torch out of a sense of purpose or they are fully aware of their diabolical malevolence caused by an insatiable lust for dictatorial power.

Either direction results from a lack of maturity, be it inadvertent or intentional, and if you trace both behaviors to the center, you will still land in the boxing ring of deception. One is deceived by their selfish desires and the other is deceived by the ones deceived by their selfish desires.

A proverbial case of the blind leading the blind.

The frustrating part of this whole "righting the wrongs" of society is getting those who you are trying to inform of these atrocities to jump the ship they have sunk their life savings into for an executive penthouse suite they purchased from their favorite local snake oil salesmen.

Hopefully, the pleas for a better cognitive reality won't fall too much on the busted eardrums of good but naïve people.

Rinse The Soap Out Of Your Brainwash

One Sided Stories are Only Half Stories

If you're only open to listening to a one-sided story, you only get half of the truth ... but if you only have half the truth, do you know if that half is the best half, an altered truth, or even the truth at all?

INFLUENCED BY CONDITIONING

If you have a group of twenty people all writing about one project to release to the public; let's say it's all chauvinistic men. Then, in addition, we have another set of only four people who are editing for the final piece of content to be released to the public; let's say they are all chauvinistic women.

What do you think the outcome would look like?

It doesn't matter what most of the writers believe; it all boils down to who's in charge of editing and releasing the final pieces of information that hold the greatest influence.

That being said, if you research, for instance, your political information from sources that are edited for public consumption by a media group that is owned by an organization that leans heavily toward right-wing or left-wing policies, the outcome will be the information that they want you to see, and omitting anything that will influence you in the other direction, which will reinforce the way you already think and believe.

Have you heard the saying: *"If all you have is a hammer, everything looks like a nail?"*

Some meanings behind this statement are:

- With limited tools, single-minded people apply them inappropriately or indiscriminately.

- If a person is familiar with a certain single subject or has a single instrument, they may have a confirmation bias to believe it's the answer to everything.

What is confirmation bias?

You believe what you believe and will find any means possible to keep that belief with a closed mind and an unwillingness to change it. Even if you have absolute facts right in front of you, you will continue to adhere to total lies simply because you're either deceived to believe the lie as being true, or you just don't want to believe the truth because it doesn't fit with what you want to believe.

This is the case in just about everything on earth that has anything to do with anything; not just politics, but religions, cultures, and entire worldviews as well. So if you don't pull from every opposing view to come to educated conclusions with the least bias and best possible outcome, you will stay stuck in the same bubble of thought that you've been in until you're open to someone or something challenging your paradigm.

I directed the point of this article at the polarization of the political arena. Hopefully, this comparison will get some to see things differently simply by flipping the coin over to open your mind to, as Paul Harvey put it... "The Rest of the Story."

For instance:

I love nature and wildlife photography, so throughout the years, I have gathered cameras and lenses to capture everything that caught my eye. I noticed that every time I had my camera with me, I would constantly be scanning the horizon for the perfect scenic landscape to capture and everything else was virtually non-existent.

I also loved sketching, so whenever I had a sketch pad and a drawing pencil, I was always attracted to something I could be drawing, paying close attention to the highlights, shadows, and fine details that would have been missed if I hadn't had a sketch pad.

Whatever I was doing or focusing on was what I was engrossed in at the time and I only noticed similar things within a very fine line on either side of that focus. This works with everything you're engaged in daily because of a "gatekeeper" in our minds called the reticular activating system. Its job is to filter out all the things that you deem to be "non-important." But ... It also doesn't care if it's right or wrong, good or bad, positive or negative ... Just that you think it's important. This explains your negative self-talk when you ask yourself the questions: *"Why does everything bad always happen to me?"* or *"Why can't I ever catch a break?"*

Your mind recognizes that those are the questions you are seeking, so it will do everything it can to let them through the gate and point out everything around you why those questions are true, and simultaneously revealing to someone else right next to you why their life is so awesome.

So … Ask better questions and focus on better solutions.

With that in mind, looking back, how many times have you noticed that whatever mood you were in, you could always find something to enhance it, or what you were concentrating on was everywhere, like … if you just bought a new vehicle, you now notice similar vehicles all over the road.

This is how the mind was created to work so in most everyday routines and tasks, this can be of great benefit for critical thinking and digging into the truth of any matter, but if your needle is stuck in the same groove, your "truth" will already be written in stone … which isn't necessarily the actual truth, but more in line with your conformation biases that have been mistaken for the truth.

***

If I were to make a suggestion, it would be to challenge yourself by looking at every point of view with the mindset that you could be wrong, (not insecure but curious) and if you are, be open to fixing it to become better educated.

Hanging on tightly to the things you've believed just because it's the way you've always believed, or been raised or taught to believe, will only keep you locked in the never-ending loop of confirmation bias.

Another parallel rabbit hole you might be interested in if you are open to that one ... is self-fulfilling prophecies. Search on those topics to get a better understanding of why you might be stuck in circular reasoning ... another way of arguing that doesn't provide any significant proof, you blindly trust simply because it's something you already believe.

This is a subject that will open up many doors and will keep you as busy as you want to be. Pace yourself when researching, but remember to keep an open mind to being wrong.

It's the only way you will grow and expand your understanding.

Indoctrinated Prejudices

The Blind Leading The Blind

Time to grow up and remove your "eye" masks!
We're encouraged to be divided over color, political bias, personal gender preferences, or sexual orientation. We're encouraged to disrespect someone who doesn't share our opinions about whether we believe we should or shouldn't blindly follow one-sided corruption institutions that spread fear and hatred, willfully complying with their control issues.

If you are in question about which side you are on ... ask yourself a question when presented with a view you don't agree with:

"What is my first concern when someone doesn't agree with my perception of the truth?"

1. To let them disagree with you with the same love and respect you demand from them about you disagreeing with them and get on with your day unhindered by that disagreement.

Or

2. To call them names and demand they comply with what you understand to be true, piss and moan about how those non-compliant little &$&^&@&$, (fill in your preferred slur here) should just do what they're told.

You be your own judge, but instead of assuming you're always right ... take an honest glance at your automatic reactionary responses to those who don't share your views without first justifying your habitual emotionally driven behavior.

Seriously!

If you've ever said that the "Republicans/Democrats" - "whites/blacks" - "women/men" - "cops" - "religions" or whatever group you throw into a collective cesspool of opinionated gibberish, you have racial tendencies.

There are good and bad individuals in every single group known to mankind, so stop spreading your disdain for whatever the media tells you to spread next and start doing actual research on what's real or not. Stop attaching yourself to a political party and automatically disagree with everything the other side has to say because you don't want to be associated with a different point of view.

If you truly want to fight against hatred, racism, and the evil things people do, fight against the oligarchs at the top who orchestrate these acts without throwing whatever group they supposedly represent into your human wood chipper. By doing so, you are spreading the same hatred inside of yourself that you are hypocritically trying to reveal in them.

It looks to me, like a worldwide pile of children fighting over the last marble on the playground; calling names because they didn't get the marble.

- "You're an idiot cuz you don't accept what I do."

- "You're a nazi, racist, homophobe because you don't think like me."

- "Put your mask on or I'm telling mommy and posting it on Facebook for the world to see how much of a pathetic slug you are and how superior I am for telling you to wear one."

- I supposedly care for your life by trying to make you comply with my standards, but then wish death to you and your family for not sharing those standards."

Suppose what you wish without the infantile bickering over what those who are NOT YOU should think and believe.

Political indoctrination you pass along on social media;

Stop ... and before you hit the "Post", "Share", or "Like" buttons, think again. It is possible to differ in views without feeling you must stir your venomous opinionated vittles into the soup.
Let whatever platform you prefer ~ be a positive way to connect and re-connect with friends and family. Stop the political garbage because ... honestly ... it's just an opinion of which side of the dung heap you choose to volley your gibberish, and by doing so you play right into the game of dividing humanity into opposing sides.

So what, you believe in something different from someone else. Change your focus, because I'll guarantee that if you try for approximately 3 seconds, you will also find common ground and many things you relate to. Compromise and move on together. If one is unwilling to compromise, move on without them, wish them well, and find someone who will.

Life is meant to live in harmony with other life. Let it be. Let grace win. We are all human. Your intellect may differ from others. Good! That means that we have something to share.
If you think your intellect is better than others, instead of using it to belittle them or make them look stupid to make yourself look smart, try the contrary. Offer it to lift them up with compassion for them. Everybody is in different places in this life. It's hard enough without adding difficulties.

Find ways to be the solution to someone's problems instead of being the problem.

Harsh Reality Of A Miserable Life

Obvious Truths Avoided Like The Plague

The quality of life is rapidly de-escalating and nobody wants to speak up. It's obvious to those who have lived a while and were raised differently than today's generations. Back then, reality was a tangible thing rather than an imaginative fantasy.

It's apparent that some don't want to live in a full state of absolute reality anymore because the truth can be offensive, but only if you're either extremely insecure, overly sensitive, or living in a victimhood mentality that generates a sense of entitlement.

The goal should be to cure people of those unrealistic states of existence rather than accepting the delusional push for a more padded alter-reality of modern-day progressive concepts called "personal truth." This is nothing more than the enabling of mental health issues that should be brought into the light of reality for a deeper state of living; but, instead, are catered to by fabricating shallow surfaces and unrealistic states of fantasy.

It doesn't help anyone. It only puts it off long enough to exist in this plastic bubble of inauthenticity and an unrealistic state of existence just to make it to bedtime so they don't have to think about life for the next few hours.

This existence only drives those who live there to alter their reality by seeking temporary ways of killing the pain of living life in a state of numbed-out hopelessness. Drugs, alcohol, excessive social media, all to gain attention by posting to get likes for the next dopamine rush to feel accepted. This includes a nonsensical illusion to identify as whatever you "feel" like on any given day.

But ...

Even though people are now encouraged to identify as whoever and whatever they aspire to be, the sad truth is that this pseudo-security blanket called their "own personal truth" changes nothing for them, as in their lives don't get any better or more fulfilling. They just continue to get more miserable and wonder if they just aren't doing "their truth" the right way. They continue to search for the next illusionary "surface-happy noun" that will somehow make life better for them.

They post more content on social media to get more attention. They create a bigger following to reach viral status to get paid more royalty revenue. They dress in the latest fad to fit in, do plastic surgery, attend popular parties ... and the list is as creative as the next big idea to avoid reality.

Unfortunately, it's a never-ending human hamster wheel that just goes around and around with no end in sight, resulting in, God forbid, suicide at unprecedented levels because of their unending states of hopelessness, wondering why this "as advertised" new and improved lifestyle isn't working for them.

They see these social media platforms displaying everyone else's life as being flawless ... After a while, they conclude that life isn't what it's all cracked up to be and lose hope that their lives will ever change. Leading to deeper depression and more and more desperate attempts to attain the peace and content happiness they desire to be a part of. Also an illusion ... because little do they know, that everyone they see on social media is just as miserable as they are, and what they post is nothing more than borrowed materialistic possessions and fake smiles. They fake happiness to get likes, comments, and shares to get a shot of endorphins to last them until the next post.

This topic can drone on and go down numerous rabbit holes that go deeper than one article can cover, so I'll make the main point of, with a bit of tweaking, this can all change, and change for the better.

To encourage the altering of reality is hurting those individuals more than it's helping and if you cared about them, you would rather encourage them to seek professional help.

Accept the truth as it is ... but ask yourself the question:

If the "TRUTH" doesn't line up with what I'm "FEELING", how can I change the "FEELING" to match that "TRUTH" instead of changing reality to match a fleeting fantasy?

Example:
1. If you "feel" depressed ... even if you've "felt" depressed from as early as you can remember ... should you accept the illusion that depression isn't curable ... or, pursue the root cause of your depression so that you can be whole and happy?

2. If you "feel" like a cat ... should you go take a dump in the

litter box ... or, dig through your emotional fantasies to see where that inkling comes from, then seek mental help as you would physical help if you broke your arm.

Know the difference between truth and imagination, or reality and fantasy. Once you have established what the truth is, determine why your feelings aren't following suit. Then work diligently on arming yourself with the wisdom necessary to align the two into one whole and complete package.

Stop listening to the brainwashed mainstream media outlets and the hijacked educational indoctrination camps. Reality is reality and truth is truth, no matter how many people are yelling out lies from the mountaintops.

Let this be your wake-up call

~ (NOT WOKE) ~

In a corrupt program full of Mr. Smiths ...
Be a Neo and break free from the Matrix.

This World Wasn't Made For You!

We Are But A Vapor

If we must cohabitate, we must learn to look outside of ourselves. The day we realize that this life wasn't built for us is the day we engage ourselves in reality.

I'm speaking of the selfishness of "us", the need to fill our pockets, barns, stomachs, houses, garages, and so on.

One day we look back on life and realize that we have surrounded ourselves with things, material possessions, items that fulfill nothing but a temporary pleasure for the times we choose to spend with them. After we put our "toys" in the garage, within minutes, the emptiness comes back in. We wander over to the refrigerator or cookie jar to momentarily fill another void, then sit in front of the television, computer, or smartphone to kill the "dead space" that would exist if our entertainment wasn't available.

One "thing" after another ... one mind-numbing event or catatonic bubble of unconsciousness after another until it's time for bed. The weekend comes and the routine changes, but the outcome is the same: A sad existence of self-gratification and a quest to "make it through another day".

Relationships are nothing more than another avenue to, again, fill our voids, never going below the surface because that would entail compromise or engagement, using them to further our agenda of self. We don't like to be alone; we need them to get more of what we want, they make our lives easier, and to justify it, we throw in a few quick "pat me on the back" duties to make ourselves look good to others, then back to our "me" routine.

If this sounds painfully familiar, here are some suggestions:

- Make it a point to engage face-to-face, instead of Facebook to Facebook.

- Spend time with friends and family, and do something for someone other than yourself.

- Schedule time to pick someone up and take them to lunch.

- Sit with someone and watch the sunset or sunrise.

- Stop and watch a bug do what it does for a few minutes.

- Practice being thankful for what you already have.

- Stop wanting others to give up their time for you and give yours to someone else.

- Take the long way home or a different way altogether.

- Listen to music in the dark while lying on the floor.

- Take a whole day and walk barefoot.

- Compliment a complete stranger.

- Pay it forward.

- Smile at everyone you see.

- Leave early and drive slowly.

- Let someone go ahead of you in line.

- When you talk to someone, listen to them and be interested in what they have to say without waiting to interject your opinion.

- Look at things through their eyes whether you agree with them or not.

- Challenge yourself to make it through an entire day without complaining about anything.

- Emphasize someone's strengths, not their weaknesses.

- Make someone laugh.

- Stop thinking about ways to make yourself happy and make someone else happy instead. You'll find that it makes you happy in the process.

- Look outside your world. There are free resources in this life called love, peace, mercy, grace, compassion, joy, etc. and the more you give away, the more you have to give. Those resources are inexhaustible and they don't cost you a dime.

- Give freely and give often.

You have the choice between good and bad, positive and negative, right and wrong, life and death ... in any and every situation, circumstance, or occasion you find yourself in.

Make the best out of this life by being conscious of every thought, action, reaction, and interaction with someone else.

Think about the best and most productive decision whenever you face another obstacle or adversity, and then make that choice to move forward.

Your life is up to you.

The more selfish you are, the more unhappy you are.

The more selfless you are, the happier you are.

It's a simple choice, but you must break those old negative conditionings you've been wallowing in and get into life.

Choose Love, Choose Life.

LIFE SUCKS!

Or ... Does It?

I hate this life; It has nothing to offer! ~ You have two ways to go from here.

You can continue to drown your sorrows with complaining, booze, drugs, or anything else that alters your so-called reality. Yes ... it might even be fun, but fun is not always good! Spend countless hours killing the time you're so opposed to being awake in, which just kicks the can of existence down the road of misery until you drift off into oblivion to get up the next morning and do it all over again.

OR

You can choose to alter your reality with a plan to make life what you would like it to be; to live it without the self-imposed deception that choice #1 is ever going to change things for the better.

Choice #1

A delusional projection that if you just kill your cognition enough to escape reality, even if it's only until the next "high" ... if you repeatedly do that enough times, somehow life will eventually fall into place and everything will be good.

~ FACT ~

This way of thinking will only cause more regrets ... which will cause more unhappiness ... causing even more misery ... complaining ... the drive to "kill the inner pain" ... more mind-altering substances ... more time-sucking activities to escape reality ... reinforcing this illusionary cesspool eddy you appear to be destined to swirl around in for eternity.

Circling right back to the beginning ... LIFE SUCKS ... I hate life ... It has nothing to offer! ... But, this time it's 10 years later ... and another 10 ... Do you see the pattern forming here?

You must stop and consciously decide to grow out of that way of thinking, which is:

Choice #2

A more solid and realistic projection to actually make things "good." To present what it means for you to be living your life inside the definition of true happiness. To live in peace, to be in harmony with everyone and everything around you, to look forward to getting up in the morning because you are the one in charge of your life instead of this life being in charge of you.

This way takes more faith to face the fears keeping you imprisoned in the endless excuses of why you can't change your circumstances. To crawl into the deep, dark, and damp caves that house the dragons you keep fighting with, those excuses you keep hiding behind. Drag them all out into the light so you can see how harmless they are.

Ask yourself a question: *"If I can't stand life anyway and feel like dying, what do I have to lose if I fight my dragons and they kill me?"*

At least ... you'll die with dignity knowing that you gave it your best shot to face what was seemingly holding you back, instead of killing yourself with the "pity cocktails" you keep making out with! At best ... you'll victoriously defeat your dragons and end up living the life you've been dreaming about!

Ask yourself another question: *"What do I have to lose?"*

The only thing keeping you stuck between choice #1 and #2 is that padded area of resistance called the unknown.

~ A.K.A. ~ THE COMFORT ZONE!

Yes ... it might be hard ... but hard is not impossible!

Ending statements for those who may need another nudge.

- Pick up that can you've been kicking down the road and turn it back in for a refund. (define your "can")

- Buy the bull, grab'em by the horns, and twist'em into submission. (define your "bull")

- Melt down your chains of complacency, beat it into a

sword, pull a dragon out of one of those caves, saddle it up, and ride that cantankerous little hussy into the sunset.

- Define your chains, sword, dragon, saddle, and sunset.

Plan of attack:

- Take whatever you think is holding you back. Your fears: ~ (Can - Bull - Dragon)

- Look it in the eyes. Bring it out into the light and face it.

- Accept it for what it is. Knowing the deepest reality is that avoiding it will NOT make it go away.

- Come up with a plan. Decide what the most productive way forward is to move past it.

- Execute! (put that plan into action)

- Expect opposition. Course correct when you hit a snag, they won't lay down without a fight.

- Celebrate your victories. (no matter how small, give yourself some credit for making the harder choice)

- Learn from your mistakes. Notice I didn't say "failures" - there are none! - take the wisdom from a "mistake" and apply it to the next challenge.

NEVER STOP

Repeat the process, and enjoy the journey.

Live life as an adventure, not a drama.

Always take time to stop and watch the sunrise/sunset, watch a butterfly, learn something you have to dig a bit to uncover, help a random stranger, lay in the grass, and watch the clouds go by.

Experiment;
Invent a new flavor by mixing something that doesn't even make sense ... place your idea here ... and here ... and here ... Go!

There is a healthy balance to life.

Take the harder ideas written above, coupled with the ending suggestions of your making, and go put your signature on the life that's been gifted to you by writing your own story!

Overpowering Deceptive Forces

Distinguishing Between The Two

Rape, theft, murder, torture, sex trafficking ... these things are noble things to fight against if you are on the side of good, but, in and of themselves, they all fit into just one category on the spectrum of behavioral influences.

You may have a list of things to either fight for or against, depending on which side of the fence you choose your battles from, but everything on earth, as far as causes go, can all be boiled down into one of two different influential forces.

GOOD OR EVIL

So, when you strap on your social injustice flag and fight against anything listed above without knowing what force you're fighting against, you will exhaust yourself thinking you're doing the right thing.

If you choose to fight for good, you invariably should fight against all evils! ... right? In your life's little circle as well as around the world. You can't picket against one without picketing against all. Otherwise, you are standing on the fence and lenient against certain other evils you choose to turn a blind eye to.

Choose a side and sell yourself to the entire cause. Not just the ones that benefit your personal convictions.

For those who fight for the evil side of things, let me give you fair warning ... good will always overpower evil. It may appear to be winning on a majority of fronts, but it will always win in the end.

The reason evil appears to be the dominant force is that those who claim to be good, stand and watch it happen without wanting to get involved. They will throw out a positive post on social media every once in a while and label themselves as a social warrior for justice; setting up camp in the field of delusional self-righteousness.

Evil is aggressive and controlling. Have you ever heard the phrase; *"There's no rest for the wicked?"* ... It means that evil doesn't rest. It's insatiably driven by lust, power, and greed and will never stop until it's satisfied ... but here's the thing ... it will never be satisfied! It will never stop! It's deceived into believing that, "the next thing," whatever that is, will be the "one" that satisfies ... to no avail.

The other deceptive side of the same coin is that good presents itself as passive and weak, and if you're a good person, you won't fight back ... Nonsense! Good is not weak; it's tremendously more powerful than evil; that is, if it chooses to fight against it! Good will always prevail against evil, as the light will always conquer darkness.

If you turn on the light, the darkness immediately dissipates into the shadows. Darkness doesn't have a switch. Evil knows this, so it tries to shut down the truths, the lights, and the goods of life.

It deceives its own workers of iniquity to maintain a shroud of darkness that says they are the most powerful ones. They stay in the shadows like cowards. They can't show their faces for fear of being snuffed out because their deeds are deserving of death. They're afraid of the light. They can't face it because their power only works in darkness. Their egotistical, insatiable arrogance blinds them into thinking they're so important that they can't mingle with the general public.

This is their justification for cowering in the shadows while they employ others to do their dirty work.

They ... Who are "they"? They are the oligarchs, some refer to them as the elites. The ones orchestrating a one-world government, a one-world religion, and a one-world reduced population. A small handful of individuals who have private meetings around the world, steer the way events unfold and financially manipulate world leaders into compliance with their agenda. They are evil to the core, causing division so they can stay hidden behind their smoke screens. Those who speak against them will be labeled as crazy conspiracy theorists. This is just another way to continue to hold power as long as they can with the least amount of static.

- Evil likes to disguise itself as good, slipping in the tiniest of truths mixed within its abundance of lies to hide its true intentions and throw you off track long enough to gain the upper hand.

- They're deceptive in all their ways with the end goal of killing, stealing, and destroying those who represent any form of promoting truth.

- Seek the obvious signs from those who are shutting down others spreading the actual truth, not the arbitrary truth. Those who speak against a life of purity, and doing the right thing. (righteousness)

- Those who promote lawlessness ... Defund police, open the borders to trafficking and drugs and judge those who have different skin tones, beliefs, or ethnicities.

- Those who want to dominate their own freedom of speech while shutting down anyone else who doesn't agree with them, (Cancel Culture) then shame those who don't comply with their indoctrination by calling them names like homophobe, white supremacist, xenophobe, nazi, racist, and whatever else they script you to say.

- Those who advocate selfishness and want to harness your free will ... wear a mask, stay inside and isolated, manipulate and force vaccinations, false political or personal "science", confusing real science.

- Those who promote sexual promiscuity and try to shut down the natural family structure by labeling it a progressive change of the times.

- Promoting unnatural unions and the illusion that you can magically choose to turn yourself into whatever you wish simply by claiming an identity.

- Advocating confusion and separation from reality to tell you that you can make up your own reality, you can claim to be an animal, women can claim to be men, men can claim to be a woman and somehow verbalizing this makes it so.

- These people have feelings and emotions, dreams and aspirations for life, they should be brought back into harmony with reality, not encouraged to embrace a chemical imbalance to further their delusional confusion.

- Caring means telling the harsh truths inside the bounds of reality, not enabling someone to live a life of constantly chasing unrealistic fantasies of perpetual euphoria.

- The ultimate goal is to abolish the very anchor point of morality and truth by implementing a system that reduces you to a purposeless lump of random cells that arranged themselves into existence for no reason at all. (EVIL'ution)

To those with eyes to see and ears to hear, it's as plain as day. To those who are blind and deceived, it's just another day in the life that changes with every wind of doctrine that blows into town.

Frogs that are in a pot with the temperature slowly increasing will stay there until they boil to death. While the pot is getting hotter, they blame the heat on their opposition and until they take their last breath, will continue to call you hateful and intolerant against those who choose to embrace this illusion.

This is no fault of those who are innocently taking part with the best of intentions. Disguised as tolerance and love, the deception towards humanity is full of hatred and disgust on the inside. Preaching freedom to live life as you wish, knowing full well that a life left unchecked by a solid moral structure will always end in suffering and death. They don't wish to see you live, they wish to dominate by diminishing the population into manageable consumers.

Everyone knows there is physical blindness, but few know of mental or spiritual blindness. If you are spiritually blind, you will continue to stand on the side of this corrupt world system, deceptively following everything that the corrupt system presents as being the "good" thing, and fall for every pill they feed you as being law while they take away one freedom at a time until there isn't any left.

Crafty and deceptive, they feed you positive and caring words like; "love is love" ~or~ "black lives matter" ... Even though love **IS** love and black lives **DO** matter, they use those phrases, not as truth, but as surface bait, to hook you into promoting their agenda, while staying behind the scenes using those hollow words to feed their insatiable lust for power, as you march with picket signs in hand, thinking you're doing your part to save the world.

If you have true sight, this world system, and everything they offer, will be a disgusting stench and despicable to you.

Don't be fooled by their crafty words telling you those who speak against you, somehow hate you, when what they are speaking against are the lies and deception keeping you blind.

Hatred toward evil, corruption, greed, selfishness, arrogance, falsehood, and the like are the actual targets ... not human beings.

How do you tell if you are blind to the evils of this world system?

Spiritual Blindness

If someone is blind from birth, you can tell them they are blind, but they have no reference for sight to even understand what that means.
A physically blind person who has never experienced physical sight can say that they understand what it means to see, but can't comprehend what the absolute truth of physical sight is ... so they remain blind.

Now, if by some miracle of fate, they receive their sight and experience what it means to physically see, it's only then that they can authentically say that they can see because now they have a reference to understand the experience of both blindness and sight. Now they can truthfully say, "I was blind, but now I see."

It's the same with mental and spiritual blindness.

If you have not experienced both spiritual blindness and spiritual sight, you remain in spiritual darkness.

You can practice yoga and inner spirituality, or attend a building called church your entire life. You can attend religious events, concerts, and bible studies, and listen to those around you talk about spiritual sight, but if you don't have a solid reference for both, frankly, you are still blind and in spiritual darkness.

Some have miraculously been given their sight, experiencing and knowing firsthand that can say they were blind. For those who say they can see without a clear time in their lives, they can emphasize as the time they received their true sight ... they remain in darkness.

This isn't a solicitation for religion or to join some cult. It's just the cold hard facts of reality and if you have never experienced it, you believe the ones who have experienced it have lost their minds by drinking the Cool Aid. But ... The "crazy" thing is, it's not difficult to be able to claim this for yourself. The most difficult thing about it is; reconditioning your mind to accept it.

It all boils down to letting go. Let go of all control, let go of your feelings and emotions ... but keep your feelings and emotions, which means flip everything around by controlling your emotions instead of them controlling you.

Swallow your selfish pride and open yourself up to humility. Most look for how others are wrong ... flip it ... look for how you are wrong.
Most see things for what they want them to be ... flip it ... see things for what they are.

Control is what flips everything around. The more control you seek, the more out of control you are. The more control you give up the more in control you are.

Separate the people, places, things, circumstances, events, happenings, and so on, from your reactions, feelings, and emotions. Let people say and do what they say and do. Let events unfold the way they will. Let circumstances be what they are. Total acceptance. It is what it is. With that comes peace, knowing that your reactions or emotions are not automatically attached to anything but your ability to regulate them at will.

Once you figure this out and learn how to let go and actually be in control of who you are ... no one will be able to push your buttons or throw you off your game.

If you're still dealing with anger, arguments, stress, anxiety, hatred, bitterness, unforgiveness, and the like ... you can be assured that you are still stuck in the matrix of spiritual blindness.

The "theys" of this world will no longer be able to create division by steering your emotions where they want them to go because you will now truly be in control.

3
POETRY COLLECTION

EMOTIONAL EXPERIENCES ~ DEEP THOUGHTS ~ LONGINGS

For no apparent reason and out of the blue,

words call out and climb into line, destined to be etched in stone.

I put my fingers on the keyboard to answer the call,

thoughts disappear into time and behold ... another poem.

This section is a compilation of the musings of the mind that seem
to be like uninvited guests that barge in and make themselves
at home, rummage through the fridge, sink into the couch, put
their feet on the coffee table, and settle in for a movie ... then you
realize, they're just part of a random guest list you made when you
were a drunk teenager.

Invisible Untapped Potential

Depth of Longing

Where are all the parameters in the scope of reality?
Does anyone know where the bottom of wisdom resides?

Can anyone comprehend to what extent the waters of
understanding flow? Is there a realization of the raw potential
for height, width, and depth?

The human mind is capable of vast expressions of imagination
that far exceed the everyday mundane droning of routine,
or carrying on throughout the day's ever-expanding cage of
existence to the tune of familiar boredom.

Drowning out the expressions of how shallow the ocean of
life is without the embrace of an intellectual encounter that
penetrates beyond the shoreline conditionings of expected
minimalistic stimulation.

Living with just enough hopeful curiosity to stay alive long
enough to see what the light of tomorrow sheds, is no place
one prefers to frequent.

Where are the deep-sea embraces that won't settle for surface
conversation? Someone tell me how to survive apart from a

longing for new adventures, the unrehearsed expectations that dwell within the imagination ...

the excitement of anticipation ...

the thrill of danger ...

and the new chapters written in this book called Life that mysteriously turn into cherished memories.

I wish to explore life's book to its fullest potential and to live the entire scope of human experience.

Word by word and cover to cover until every page has been exhausted by the dance of blissful encounter.

I desire to live, to love, and enjoy every breath that the source of everything alive has gifted me

and all of this to share with the one created to embody the other half of my soul.

Together

Forever as one.

Silent Cries

Desperation of an Empty Soul

Silent and lonely screaming is unfortunately the way of those who live with no real functioning means of verbal expression, alone and desperately grasping for approval, imprisoned words locked in a dungeon with the keys just out of reach.

Hoping, praying, and wishing with every fiber of being for a single miracle that just happens ...

as random favor ... just because ...

or anything else that might volunteer in the process toward freedom from the inner chambers of a restless soul.

Silence is the biggest fan base in this echo chamber that plays on the strings of the heart.

Endless rehearsals to perform concerts of unheard masterpieces in empty spaces to faceless faces ...

hoping one day ... someone ... somewhere ...

will decipher this immortal symphony of silent cries.

To break free from the heavy chains of desperation for real

connection, way beyond the surface mundane routine and hollow thoughts that plague the mind with stale ramblings in off-key tunes of outdated memories.

Wide open for change ... lasting change ...

to wander in fields of vast and plentiful splendor, unending bliss, and deep contentment that's as thick as the crust of the earth ...

to mesh with this existence as if time, space, and matter were all one unit that extends far past eternity.

To play a new song of bright melodies and the harmonious whispers of angelic voices ringing clear with fresh beginnings ...

living in a new world ... loving and being loved ...

peace that penetrates every worry like the warm summer sun in a cloudless sky, melting away anxiety to live the life that was originally intended by the source of everything alive.

* * *

I have traded in my sorrows to live in harmony with the Source of life, man, and nature.

No more empty spaces or faceless faces ...
No more cold and hardened sighs ending in lonely silent cries ...

Life is meant to live ...
Choose Love ... Choose Life ... Live Life!

Keep Your Faith Until The End

Remember your Fate

There is a way that seems right to a man,
Lies and deception to gain all that they can.
Filling their pockets with ill-gotten gain,
not a care in the world for their trail of pain.

The broken souls they leave within the force of their wake,
to pick up shattered pieces in the life they must make.

Silent cries of injustice make their way up to God,
while He prepares for the wicked deep down in the sod.

Keeping the faith through the thick and the thin,
because in the end the deceivers and the like will not win.

Keeping the faith through the suffering and pain,
because in the end, it's the doers of right that will abundantly gain.

Gaining everything back that was stolen or lost,
the reward that awaits will by far pass the cost.

If the pounding waves of this life have beaten you down,
just remember that this place isn't all that there is,
continue in gratitude, peace, joy, and in love,
keep your focus on the eternal because the temporal will fizz.

My Brothers Keeper

We are all as one

Who is my brother but an extension of I,
no shape, no color, or physical space,
a job, a profession, or another blank face.

Not a weakness, a worthless, or a stumbling fraud,
nor performance, or action, not here or abroad.

We're not separated by space, or matter and time,
nor money, or status, they do not define,
our eternal worth and strength or who it is that we are,
our core should exceed all those things, and by far.

Take away this body in physical space,
our identity, names, and the shape of our face,
the stars the moon and the warmth of the sun,
for it's inside the spirit we're all connected as one.

In that spirit, there's no indifference, blame, or division,
no fighting for power, but a conscious decision,
for a pure connection with one and another,
yes, your keeper is me ...

because you are my Brother.

Shackles Of Limitation

Once you know there's more ... Less will never satisfy

Pure unadulterated individual expression, untainted by the ego,
is blind to selfish desires. Why does the outward human intellect
disappoint the deepest parts of the inner spiritual soul?

How does one communicate an inexpressible emotion to another
soul using only the limited verbal language that falls far short of
its intended destination?

Drawing back the bowstrings of communication to release the
arrow of intent only to disrupt the smoky holographic target of
understanding that dissipates into the ever-expansive atmosphere
of relation.

Momentarily disappointed by this realistic illusion, the balanced
satisfaction of a solid connection seems to elude the bullseye
once again.

Quickly closing the gap to acceptance, I can feel in my soul that
these pseudo illusions are just the stepping stones necessary to
lead me toward what lies waiting in the patient future.

That one arrow in my quiver that will penetrate dead-center in
the heart of its final target, instantaneously melding into one as
two separate single bodies of water fuse when they touch.

Sometimes the exhausting attempts for connection leave me homeless in the village of food stamp relationships, feeding only inside the parameters of this walled-off mandated entrapment, otherwise known as physical existence.

If this flesh and blood uniform represents the darkness I must succumb to inhabit until the liberation of my soul, then let it find the means to a higher expression of language that doesn't rely on mere words, as to experience an entire conversation held within a single stare.

Reveal to me the realm of light that finds its connections in pure meaning itself. A space so expansive there are no boundaries or shackles of limitation.

Release my soul to explore the far reaches of space to experience every drop of life intended in the original divine design for humanity. No more physical illusionary limitations that keep this avatar chained to the blinded eyes of materialistic pursuits.

Fall the scales from my limited vision and dial into focus the true reality found only in the submersion of pure love.

Because ... Perfect love drives out all fear.

Cycles Of Seeking Faith

Real Faith Produces Real Peace

The truth I seek is impossible to find without a supernatural intervention ... and at times it appears that the supernatural isn't often interested in mortal endeavors.

It also appears that a quest to reside on the mountain tops ... inadvertently renders the wallowing in the cold and dreary valleys below.

I refuse to settle for a life of mediocrity which, so far has only led to disappointment and confusion.

Although it has been the crumbling default dwelling shelter, it has kept me from the extreme elements of total disparity, and the thorn in my soul that drives me to venture out beyond mortal vision ... to find the place that fits like the last shattered piece restored to a once whole masterpiece.

At one point, the double-edged sword of self-reliance must push outward to open up another form of existence that resides in a realm unknown to the physical dimension ... to put a strange concept into action called blind faith.

But, referring to it as action ... somehow implies that it originates in the physical self ... this takes back that force beyond your control and strips the meaning from the very definition of faith itself ... to place the credit back on your empty physical attempts.

When you can fully release any attachment to "self" ... and lay down a decision, a plan, or your very existence to a resting place beyond your control ... then you can feel the total peace that the core of faith offers ... as the gift of absolute surrender.

That place where the giving ... IS the receiving.

Where the letting go ... IS the solid grasp of reality.

~ AND ~

Where the dying ... IS the living.

Real Life

The Rhelm Beyond

The only feeling I long to experience is the one that fully presents itself as an incomparable reality.

An experience so deep that it takes over what can be physically felt, something surpassing reality that dwarfs the senses in comparison and replaces everything that has ever been felt so far with a sensation only experienced in the realm of imagination.

I don't want to see a sunset ... I want to feel it.

I don't want to hear a song ... I want to embody it.

I don't want to feel a gentle touch ...
I want to climb in and paint it into my being as pigment meshes with canvas ...

Making it no longer two separate entities but one complete finished masterpiece, sealed and ready for wire to be hung in the sky for the entire world to share.

There are no human words that can express what I desire to live.

The word "live" itself is the only word that can be pulled from the choices constructed by mere flesh to explain a sense of being, attempting to define an observation as another flesh being ...

I know there is something more ...
I know there is something different ...

I know there is something far beyond anything that has been expressed within the farthest reaches of mortal man ... a longing that doesn't register inside the confines of language.

Those who see these words as a simple human expression will dismiss them as a surface experience and it will end at that ... but those who can see beneath that surface will relate in a way that resonates with the original divine design ... far surpassing anything that can be expressed by man-made words or could ever be explained by the limited, human, exhaustible, library of confinement.

Every word I just uttered is a pile of filthy rags compared to what I know to be authentic reality.

I wish I could explain what is buried within my thoughts ... or express what is felt in the inner chambers of imagination.

I wish ... I wish I could delve into a language that could portray the workings of the pure untapped mind ...

I don't think I will ever be understood ...
as I wish to be understood!

Turning Cold

Pursuit of Forgiveness

Blatant deceptive disrespect after so long turns oneself cold.

Once fresh, even care can rust and crumble into dust.

Outward beauty turns into an impenetrable black veil.

Words mean nothing
without actions to fill the void that validates truth.

Living in a rut for far too long,
it really is a shame that a once-treasured existence
can slip so far away that even the hope that sewed everything
together ... without warning ...
becomes unraveled, and falls to the ground to rot.

Saving up to purchase the gear to scale Mt. Forgiveness
might just be a millionaire's task.

Grant me access to the bottomless divine vault,

because I fall far short of the funds necessary
to complete this endeavor.

So What

Why Does it Matter

So what ... you're black.   So what ... you're white.
So what ... you're a doctor. So what ... you fight.

So what ... you're bald.   So what ... you're quiet.
So what ... you're boring.   So what ... you're a riot.

So What!

None of that is the focus

On and on, on and on, I could quite easily go on forever,
about the way we carry on about who we are and chaining
ourselves to a color, a job, a gender, a weight or a height, an
ethnicity, a culture, a wrong or a right.

Whatever title we choose to identify with, that very choice
separates us from a much bigger plan.

In and of our very being, within our hearts and minds, we are not
a skin tone, a sexual preference, or even a woman or a man.

Because if we all go back in time ... In the beginning ...
to the original design,

we were all called to live with joy and harmony ...
and in peace with the Divine.

So before you plant your individual residence flag within a title or
a geographical location, a world view, a political stance, a gender,
or your day-to-day vocation,

think deeper within this thought ...

If you take away those skin tones, the different languages, or
locations on the globe, we are all stripped bare, and we are all
alike standing naked without the robe.

The robe of prejudice that separates us from connecting with
someone who doesn't see things the way we do,
or a belief we choose to close off from just because we don't
understand, so label it taboo.

Just remember that we all walk this earth one breath and one step
at a time, only getting this one life, stop wasting it with hatred,
disunity, indifference, and strife.

Because we are all members of the same race, the human race,
just different tastes and spice.
Deep down we all speak one language, and that's the language of
laughter, of love, and of life.

Anything outside of that ... So What!

Absolute Power Is Mine

Who Am I

WHO AM I

I am but a tiny vessel,
entire countries I can destroy.

I can ruin lives that last for generations,
and crush hope like a plastic toy.

WHO AM I

I can change the course of history,
like the whisper of a breath.

I have no arms or legs,
but possess the power of life and death.

WHO AM I

I am not at all physically sharp,
but I wound deeper than a knife.

I can leave internal scars that last for years,
and with the stroke of a pen, take life.

WHO AM I

I can also change life for the better,
break chains of torment and despair.

Wage war on anger, resentment, bitterness,
and a depth of love and care

WHO AM I

I can be a generous giver,
and a taker if I think I should.

I can run with the best and stand by the rest,
I can choose between evil and good.

WHO AM I

With one word I can sink a fleet of ships,
and many a man from trees I've hung.

With one word I can change the course of a life,
and my name is this ...

THE TONGUE

Within Lies the Power of Life and Death.

I would like to sincerely thank you for reading this book and I would love to know what you think.

Was it challenging, or helpful? Did you enjoy the read? I invite you to give it a star rating and an honest review either on Amazon or my website, wherever you purchased the book.

Also, if you have any questions, comments, or concerns, feel free to send me a message from the form on my Contact Page at www.rickbartrand.com

Thank you

~ Rick ~

ACKNOWLEDGEMENTS

MY RELATIONSHIP CIRCLE

Family ... Parents, siblings, cousins, nieces, and nephews who lend an encouraging word or just sit there and listen to whatever I have to say.

Friends ... Those who had a choice to stick around without the expected bond of blood to connect us, the ones that sit and chat about the deeper things of life around a campfire.

Fans ... Those on social media platforms who have liked and commented with an honest evaluation, it's most appreciated.

Corrections ... Faye Bartrand, Diane Krantz, and Pam Harvey for taking your time to sift through the jungle of verbiage to make it a bit more presentable to the public

A deep heartfelt sense of gratitude for those who, without a thought, will support me and my work without hesitation. To purchase a book just because another one was published, not because they wanted to read it, although they do anyway. :) You know who you are. Thank you so much; that means the world to me. Also, those who support me with monthly financial donations so I can continue to bring hope to those who might need that extra nudge to make it until tomorrow.

Most of all, I give thanks to the Source of Life that makes it possible for everything to exist. Without this gift of life, none of us would be here to be able to experience all the senses, emotions, and feelings to every degree on both sides of the spectrum. There is a purpose for everything under the sun.

I thank you all.

~ THANK YOU ~

Best of Luck, Many Blessings, and Much Love

If you've made it to this page, I just want to say—thank you. Truly.

Time is the most valuable thing we have, and the fact that you chose to spend some of it with my words means more than you know. Whether this book stirred something new in you, challenged your perspective, or simply gave you something to think about on a quiet afternoon ~ I am grateful that you came along for the journey.

If the content resonated with you in any way, I'd be honored if you took a few moments to head back to where you picked up this book and leave a star rating and an honest review.   *(Direct Amazon QR Code Above)*
Your words matter more than algorithms—reviews help future readers know if this book belongs in their hands too.

If you're the kind of person who enjoys chewing on life's deeper questions, and maybe even laughing a little while doing it, I'd love to stay connected. Come join the tribe of thinkers, soul-searchers, and dragon-sleighers—yes, they're real—by hopping on the newsletter.

No fluff. No spam. Just thought-provoking musings, first looks at new projects, and the occasional spark to brighten your day or ignite your mind.

You can join us at: www.rickbartrand.com (Your inbox deserves meaningful company.) Until next time … Stay curious. Stay courageous. And never stop seeking the truth.

With much gratitude;   ~ *Rick* ~

ABOUT THE AUTHOR

Rick is a truth-seeker and author who has spent decades charting the unexplored territories of the human spirit, faith, and freedom.

Born and raised in Michigan, Rick's love for the wild outdoors and quiet reflection has shaped a life devoted to uncovering timeless wisdom and sharing it with fellow authentic truth-seekers, soul warriors, and skeptics, ready to saddle dragons and ride.

From humble beginnings flipping burgers and working construction to serving his country as a U.S. Navy air-crewman on combat support helicopters, Rick's boots-on-the-ground life experience gives him raw authenticity you can feel on every page.

Richard Bartrand

He's a skilled handyman, an over-the-road truck driver, built businesses, and guided others as a thought coach, helping to reclaim inner strength and clarity.

But Rick's greatest adventure didn't come from the road or the sky, it came through a thorough analysis into self-mastery, spiritual awakening, and philosophical exploration. Over 20 years of journaling, seeking, and learning forged his voice as an author who doesn't offer fluff or feel-good clichés, but bold truths that challenge your thinking and ignite your soul.

When he's not writing, you'll find Rick capturing wildlife through a camera lens in the Michigan woods, or sharing stories beside the warm glow of a crackling campfire.

MORE BOOKS BY THIS AUTHOR

And more to come for those who dare to question, seek, and live fully awake.

PERSONAL DEVELOPMENT

BITE SIZE LIFE LESSONS
Modern-Day Proverbs * Volumes 1 & 2

VOLUME
1

VOLUME
2

BITE-SIZED REAL-WORLD WISDOM FOR EVERYDAY APPLICATIONS

From overcoming challenges to embracing change, this is your personal road-map to self-improvement, personal success, and a life of intention. Filled with practical insights, timeless wisdom, and real-world strategies, every page of Bite Size Life Lessons is designed to challenge your thinking and elevate your personal growth.

- Live with focused intention.

- Strengthen your mindset and self-awareness.

- Eye-opening revelations.

You're not just buying a book . . .

you're investing in decades of practical wisdom that can shift your thinking for the better, one page at a time.

SPIRITUAL AWAKENING

SO... YOU THINK YOU'RE AN ATHEIST
Questions That Haunt The Soul

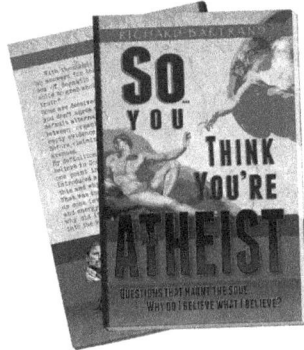

FINDING CLARITY IN BETWEEN DOGMA AND SKEPTICISM

Inside a world of conflicting beliefs and dogmatic worldviews, it often feels impossible to find answers. This is your guide to navigating these murky waters and uncovering the universal truths that lie between rigid doctrines and skeptical perspectives. Many find themselves trapped in the misconception that rejecting organized religion must automatically lead to atheism.

- Reflect deeply on your thoughts and beliefs.
- Convincing arguments don't always lead to facts.
- How logic can coexist with authentic faith

In an endless sea of worldviews ... This is your anchor buoy!

"The arduous battle through religion and atheism almost drove me insane... until I let go of both." This raw, honest journey is for those who dare to ask: "What if there's more?"

THOUGHT-PROVOKING

SMOKING THE PIPE OF CONTEMPLATION
Road To Revelation * Volume 1

A PHILOSOPHICAL JOURNEY INTO THE ABYSS OF REFLECTIVE THOUGHT.

Have you unknowingly inherited a worldview crafted by those who came before you? This isn't about telling you what to believe—it's about exploring, deconstructing, and rediscovering truth through raw personal reflections, deep philosophical inquiries, and candid takes on modern controversies, it will push you into the crater of critical thinking, self-awareness, and reflective thought.

- A spark of curiosity and mindfulness.
- Mental clarity and emotional intelligence.
- Compelling perspectives on life's meaning.

Read with an open mind. Walk away with it sharpened.

If you're ready to question, to contemplate, and to uncover deeper truths, then this book is your invitation to fire up the Pipe of Contemplation.

PLANNING / ORGANIZATION

90-DAY GOAL PLANNER
Reach Your Intended Goals

TRACK YOUR DAILY / WEEKLY PROGRESS

3 - four-week daily planners plus one week to transition into your next 90-day list of goals.

A 30-day and a 60-day checkpoint to stay on track to reach your 90-day target.

Keep your next 3 months organized with this daily / weekly / monthly / quarterly production goal planner.

- Reach your intended goals.
- Track your daily / weekly progress.
- 30 & 60 Day Production Checkpoints

A written dream attached to a date becomes a goal.

Measure progress and add accountability, it becomes a plan.

Integrate it into your daily practice and it becomes a reality.

CHILDREN'S BOOK

THE ADVENTURES OF SUZIE Q AND HATTIE SNACKS
TWIN FLAMES

AN EVERYDAY QUEST TO FIND AND EXPLORE SOMETHING NEW.

Embark on a delightful journey with Suzie Q and Hattie Snacks as they explore the wonders of their everyday world.

This colorful and imaginative children's poem cartoon book invites young readers to tag along on the twins' playful adventures around the house.

- Playful, Fun, Joyful, and Adventurous.
- Big Bold Print
- Colorful Illustrations

Your children will enjoy following along on the adventures of Suzie Q and Hattie Snacks for many years to come, with its fun and creative, bright and happy pictures along with big bold print as they learn how to read.

CONTACT INFORMATION

WEB SITE
WWW.RICKBARTRAND.COM

AMAZON AUTHOR PAGE
WWW.AMAZON.COM/AUTHOR/RICHARDBARTRAND

The Social Connection

FACEBOOK
@RICKBARTRANDTHOUGHTCOACH

INSTAGRAM
@RB_THOUGHTCOACH

LINKEDIN
@RICKBARTRAND

YOUTUBE
@RB_THOUGHTCOACH

X
@RICKBARTRAND

SEE YOU SOON!

www.ingramcontent.com/pod-product-compliance
Lightning Source LLC
Chambersburg PA
CBHW051842090426
42736CB00011B/1925